MOSES

A Man of Selfless Dedication

BIBLE STUDY GUIDE

From the Bible-teaching ministry of

CHARLES R. SWINDOLL

INSIGHT FOR LIVING

Chuck graduated in 1963 from Dallas Theological Seminary, where he now serves as the school's fourth president, helping to prepare a new generation of men and women for the ministry. Chuck has served in pastorates in three states: Massachusetts, Texas, and California, including almost twenty-three years at the First Evangelical Free Church in Fullerton, California. His sermon messages have been aired over radio since 1979 as the *Insight for Living* broadcast. A best-selling author, Chuck has written numerous books and booklets on many subjects.

Based on the outlines and transcripts of Chuck's sermons, the study guide text is co-authored by Jason Shepherd, a graduate of Texas A&M University and Dallas Theological Seminary. He also wrote the Living Insights sections and dramatic narratives.

Editor in Chief:
Cynthia Swindoll
Director, Educational Ministries:
Gary Matlack
Senior Study Guide Writer:
Jason Shepherd
Senior Editor and Assistant Writer:
Wendy Peterson
Copy Editors:
Deborah Gibbs
Marco Salazar
Glenda Schlahta

Text Designer:
Gary Lett
Graphic System Administrator:
Bob Haskins
Publishing System Specialist:
Alex Pasieka
Director, Communications Division:
John Norton
Project Coordinator:
Shannon Scharkey
Production Coordinator:
Cheri Liefeld

Unless otherwise identified, all Scripture references are from the New American Standard Bible, updated edition, copyright © The Lockman Foundation 1960, 1962, 1963, 1968, 1971, 1972, 1973, 1975, 1977, 1995. Used by permission. Scripture taken from the Holy Bible, New International Version © 1973, 1978, 1984 International Bible Society, used by permission of Zondervan Bible Publishers [NIV]. The other version cited is the New King James Version [NKJV].

ISBN 1-57972-097-8

STUDY GUIDE COVER DESIGN: Alex Pasieka. Adapted from the hardback cover design by D² Design Works; hardback illustration by David Bowers.

Printed in the United States of America

CONTENTS

* These messages were not a part of the original series but are compatible with it.

INTRODUCTION

Moses . . . just reading that name sends my mind spinning into orbit!

He was born after midnight in the history of the Hebrews . . . found by Pharaoh's daughter in the Nile . . . nurtured at his mother's breast for only a few precious years before being deposited into the pagan culture of Egypt. Impulsive and rash in his attempt to help his people, he fled to the desert with murder on his record—fully convinced he was a washout. He married, watched his father-in-law's flock, and endured forty years of obscurity, solitude, and silence as God remade and readied him to deliver God's people God's way in the epochal event of the Exodus.

You and I will have little difficulty identifying with Moses' frustrations and failures. Nor will we struggle trying to understand the pain of being "shelved" for an extended period of time. But we'll be thrilled to hear again that our God is still in the business of using broken and scarred vessels to accomplish His plan.

Moses . . . he, being dead, still speaks! As you study with us, be ready to obey God's voice. It is loud and clear.

Chuck Swindoll

Chuck Swindoll

PUTTING TRUTH
INTO ACTION

K nowledge apart from application falls short of God's desire for His children. He wants us to apply what we learn so that we will change and grow. This study guide was prepared with these goals in mind. As you go through the following pages, we hope your desire to discover biblical truth will grow as your understanding of God's Word increases and that you will be encouraged to apply what you've learned.

To assist you in your study, we've included a section called **Living Insights** at the end of each lesson. These exercises will challenge you to study further and to think of specific ways to put your discoveries into action.

On occasion a lesson is followed by a **Digging Deeper** section, which gives you additional information and resources to probe further into some issues raised in that lesson.

There are many ways to use this guide—in personal devotions, group studies, discussions with friends and family, and Sunday school classes. And, of course, it's an ideal study aid when you're listening to its corresponding *Insight for Living* radio series.

To benefit most from this study guide, we would encourage you to consider it a spiritual journal. That's why we've included space in the **Living Insights** for recording your thoughts and discoveries. We hope you'll return to those sections often for review and encouragement as you continue to grow in your walk with Christ.

Jason Shepherd
Coauthor of Text
Author of Living Insights
Author of Dramatic Narratives

MOSES

A Man of Selfless Dedication

PANORAMA OF MOSES' LIFE

	The First Forty Years	The Second Forty Years	The Third Forty Years
The Lesson	Thinking He Was Somebody	Learning He Was Nobody	Discovering What God Could Do with a Nobody
The Location	EGYPT	MIDIAN	EGYPT, WILDERNESS
Key Elements	• Nursed at home • Schooled . . . skilled • Self-willed, impatient • Fled for his life	• Father, shepherd, servant • Alone . . . broken • Humble . . . sensitive • Useful to God	• Deliverance of Hebrew people • The Law • The Tabernacle • Wanderings
	Exod. 1:1–2:15; Acts 7:17– 29a	*Exod. 2:16–4:28; Acts 7:29b – 34*	*Exod. 4:29 – Deut. 34:12; Acts 7:35 – 44*

NOTE: Based on Acts 7:23, 30 and Deuteronomy 34:7, we can divide Moses' life into three forty-year segments.

THE LAND OF MOSES' LIFE

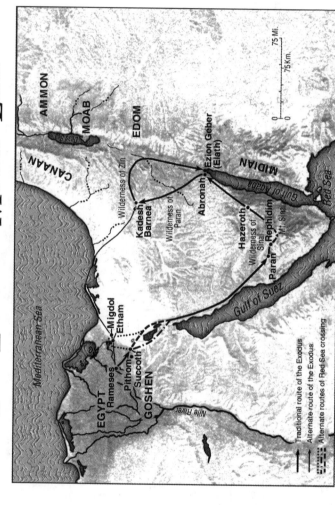

Nelson's Complete Book of Bible Maps and Charts: Old and New Testaments (Nashville, Tenn.: Thomas Nelson Publishers, 1993), p. 31. Used by permission of Thomas Nelson, Inc.

EXPLANATION OF DIFFERENCES READER WILL SEE IN THIS GUIDE

You never really know someone until you live with them.

Anyone who has lived with a roommate or spouse will testify to the truth of that statement. To completely understand other people, you have to enter their world and take into account the surroundings in which they live. Historic figures are especially hard to understand because they and their world have passed away. But if we can enter their lives through stories and gain more knowledge about their cultures, we stand a better chance of knowing them the way they really were.

This is certainly true of Moses. His education in Egypt acted like an anvil on which his character was pounded out. And the slavery of his people served as a fire, tempering his values. As a result, Moses hated oppression and fought against injustice throughout his life. We've filled this guide with dramatic narratives that allow us into Moses' world, giving us a clearer picture of the era into which he was born. Through these scenes, we will know him like we've never known him before. He will become a living, breathing, flesh-and-bone man.

Chapter 1

MISERY, MIDWIVES, AND MURDER

Exodus 1

What do you do in a no-win situation? Like walking through a dark room, it seems as though the question is not, "Will you stub your toe?" but, "When?" One wrong, inevitable misstep turns your fears into reality, and you've got a throbbing pain shooting from your toe to your shin. The only preparation you can make as you walk is to convince yourself that, although the pain will come, it will also pass. Before Moses' birth, the Hebrew slaves must have felt a similar, although much more ominous, sense of impending doom as they lived in Egypt. They knew that Pharaoh hated them and that the Egyptians despised them. Only time would reveal when the other shoe would drop.

Inside the throne room of his palace, Pharaoh looked with disgust at the supplicant who had come to beg mercy. Accused of stealing Egyptian livestock, he was a *shasu*—a wanderer, one of the few Hebrews whom Pharaoh still allowed to herd sheep and goats. The rest had been forced into hard labor building Egypt's fortune cities—and rightfully so, based on what Pharaoh was now seeing: a grizzled Hebrew thief covered with goat-smell. With an apathetic flick of the back of Pharaoh's hand, the blubbering Hebrew was dragged out of the room by two thick-bodied guards.

Pharaoh brooded on his throne. "What are we going to do about all these repugnant Hebrews?" he asked, looking at the flock of advisers hovering in one corner. "Nothing we try works. They breed like insects. For every one we kill, two take its place."

"Please allow me, your majesty," one of the men said as he stepped forward. The palace priest-physician was a tall, lean man with an uncommon fluidity and smoothness in the way he moved. "May I repeat the proposal I presented a few days ago?" he asked.

"I remember it," Pharaoh said. "It's sounding better all the time. Summon the midwives."

"Actually, sir, I anticipated this time would come. They're waiting in the chamber. Will you see them now?"

Pharaoh thought a moment, then nodded. A guard ushered in Shiphrah and Puah, two Hebrew midwives who had been waiting in the palace court-yard. They prostrated themselves before the king.

"Rise," Pharaoh said.

The women lifted their hard-worn bodies from the floor. They tried not to make eye contact but also tried not to look like they were avoiding it. To meet Pharaoh's eyes brought death to a Hebrew slave. But to avoid them encouraged suspicion, which often led to death as well.

"You have nothing to fear," he said. "If you do what you're told."

Pharaoh waved for the priest-physician to

come over. Shiphrah knew about him and greatly admired him because there was no one more talented in the medical arts in all of Egypt.

"I'm going to show you a new technique," he said, as Shiphrah listened intently. "When the baby emerges from the birth canal, support its head with one of your hands." He held his hand out and cupped it with the palm up, the long, gentle fingers cradling an imaginary cranium. "Place your palm under the back of the baby's head like this, and use your fingers to support the shoulders and upper back."

"Pardon me, sir," Shiphrah said, "but wouldn't two hands be safer?"

"No. You'll need the other hand for something else." Then he continued his explanation. "As the child comes further out, look to see what sex it is. If it's a girl, use your second hand to support the bottom until the rest of the body leaves the canal." He placed his hand as though he was supporting the rest of the body. "Then continue as you always do."

"What if it's a boy?" she asked, wondering why the baby's sex made a difference.

"If it's a boy, take your other hand and wrap it around the front of the child's head," he angled the other hand in the air positioning the imaginary head between his palms. Shiphrah noticed how his hands moved with the agility and swiftness of an artist. He was good. Very good.

"Then what do we do?" she said, quivers of agitation beginning to ripple in her voice. "When the rest of the body emerges, it will dangle from our hands, which could cause all kinds of damage . . ."

3

The priest-physician's glare silenced Shiphrah immediately. "Before the boy takes his first breath," he continued, "you will clasp your hand around his mouth and clamp his nostrils with your fingers, suffocating him." Once again he demonstrated the procedure, but this time the skill and precision of his movements struck a deep fear in Shiphrah. "All Hebrew boys must die," he intoned. "Pharaoh has declared it."

She couldn't believe what she was hearing. He was supposed to be a healer, not a murderer. How could he even propose such a thing? She turned to Puah, now a pale, ghostly color.

"You will teach this technique to the other midwives," Pharaoh commanded. "No Hebrew boy can live; I want each one dead before he ever draws his first breath."

Pharaoh dismissed the midwives with another apathetic flick of his hand, and the guards hustled the women out, who were finding it hard to walk under their own strength.

The History of the Problem

What a slap in the face to the Hebrews' already miserable existence! Pharaoh, as though he wanted to rub salt in an open lash-mark, heaped death upon their pain. Before we explore the rest of the story, though, we need to look back several hundred years to fully understand Pharaoh's animosity toward the people of Israel.

Arrival in Egypt

Almost four hundred years before the birth of Moses, the patriarch Joseph was born to Jacob. Unfortunately, Jacob's intense love for this son drove the others to jealousy, and they despised him (Gen. 37:3–4). They threw him into a pit and sold him to a group of traders, who sold him to Potiphar, the captain of Pharaoh's bodyguard, in Egypt (vv. 18–36). After some roller-coaster years, in which his early successes were rewarded with injustice and neglect, Joseph was finally elevated to Egypt's prime minister. In that role, he answered only to Pharaoh (41:38–44).

During the first seven years of his reign, Joseph executed a grain storage plan that prepared Egypt for a great famine that would devastate the whole region[1] (vv. 28–32, 46–49). When the famine hit, "people of all the earth came to Egypt to buy grain from Joseph" (v. 57). This very catastrophe led Joseph's family to leave Canaan and eventually be reunited with him. Pharaoh, out of gratitude for the good Joseph did for the empire, granted him one of the finest spreads of land in Egypt, a place called Goshen (47:5–6). Joseph accepted the offer and moved his family there.

Prosperity in Egypt

As time passed, Jacob's family became richer and acquired more land in Goshen. His clan also began to multiply as his sons married and bore children (v. 27). This economic and familial growth continued unabated for hundreds of years. When Moses finally arrived on the scene, the Hebrews had become "exceedingly mighty, so that the land was filled with them" (Exod. 1:7 NIV).

Brutality in Egypt

Unlike previous pharaohs, the one who ruled Egypt at the time of Moses' birth knew nothing about Joseph and his service to the Egyptian empire (v. 8). This king hated the Hebrews because he feared they would turn against the Egyptians and join their enemies, plundering Egypt's wealth. Even with Pharaoh's mighty army, the

---

1. Verse 56 says that the famine affected "all the face of the earth," which, rather than indicating a global famine, probably meant "the known world from the writer's perspective (the Middle East). This description of the famine in the time of Joseph echoes the author's description of the flood in the time of Noah. God saved only Noah and his family from the flood, so that Noah became the new (after Adam) father of the race. With the call of Abram out of the post-flood and post-Babel nations, God once more singled out one man, now to be the father of his special people. God promised that, through this man and his descendants, 'all peoples on earth will be blessed' (12:3). The author highlights the fact that in this new crisis hope rested with one of these descendants." Ronald Youngblood, note on Genesis 41:57, in *The NIV Study Bible*, gen. ed. Kenneth L. Barker (Grand Rapids, Mich.: Zondervan Bible Publishers, 1985), p. 69.

5

Hebrews had the sheer numbers to make it happen.

Pharaoh's fear soon festered into brutality, and he instituted a campaign of oppression.

> So they appointed taskmasters over them to afflict them with hard labor. And they built for Pharaoh storage cities, Pithom and Raamses. But the more they afflicted them, the more they multiplied and the more they spread out, so that they were in dread of the sons of Israel. The Egyptians compelled the sons of Israel to labor rigorously; and they made their lives bitter with hard labor in mortar and bricks and at all kinds of labor in the field, all their labors which they rigorously imposed on them. (vv. 11–14)

When this strategy failed, Pharaoh then turned to his priest-physician for help.

God's Promise of Deliverance

Although Joseph's prosperity and success had turned into slavery and brutality, Israel still had a divine promise to cling to. They had these words from Yahweh to Abraham:

> "Know for certain that your descendants will be strangers in a land that is not theirs, where they will be enslaved and oppressed four hundred years. But I will also judge the nation whom they will serve, and afterward they will come out with many possessions." (Gen. 15:13–14)

Their trial had been long and harsh, but it would not last forever. God promised deliverance, and as we'll now see, He started to till the hard, fallow ground of slavery with the courageous actions of two brave midwives.

The Midwives' Response

Pharaoh's command to kill Israel's baby boys appalled the midwives. Once the gravity of the situation had settled in, Shiphrah and Puah knew there was only one thing to do.

> But the midwives feared God, and did not do as the king of Egypt had commanded them, but let the boys live. (Exod. 1:17)

6

Not getting the results he wanted, Pharaoh called the midwives back to the palace. "Why have you done this thing, and let the boys live?" he interrogated (v. 18). They answered:

> "Because the Hebrew women are not as the Egyptian women; for they are vigorous and give birth before the midwife can get to them." . . . And the people multiplied, and became very mighty. (vv. 19, 20b)

Were the midwives telling the truth? Did Pharaoh believe their excuse? We don't know. But we do know that Pharaoh abandoned his scheme with the midwives and moved on to another, more brutal plan.

> Then Pharaoh commanded all his people, saying, "Every son who is born you are to cast into the Nile, and every daughter you are to keep alive." (v. 22)

A mass drowning of all the little boys. If Pharaoh couldn't suffocate them fresh from the womb, he would sink them in the river.

Four Timeless Principles

What an inhuman plan! What desperate times. But not hopeless. For even amid the darkness of Pharaoh's tyranny flickered the light of God's presence and promise. A light that gave the Hebrews hope, encouragement, and direction. A light that shines for us as well. Four principles stand out from the Hebrews' response to Pharaoh's decree.

Submitting to Civil Authority Has Limits

Have you ever been taught that "good Christians" must do whatever an authority requires, regardless of the circumstances? People who adhere to this idea believe that no matter who the authority is or what he or she commands, the ethical response is to comply. It's a blanket submission mentality that covers every relationship in life.

Pharaoh was an authority over the midwives, and he gave them a command. But the midwives weren't blanket submitters. Not only did they refuse to obey him, they most likely covered up their rebellion with a lie. Now some people may read this verse and think, "Well, God wouldn't honor that kind of behavior." But verses 20–21 reveal that He did honor them:

> So God was good to the midwives. . . . Because the midwives feared God, He established households for them.

Does God honor sin, then? No, but He does bless the greater good. Before we go any further, let's put some reins on this principle so we don't take it too far. This passage does not teach children to disobey or deceive their parents, wives to usurp their husbands' leadership in the home, or anyone to reject ethical authority or to lie. But the passage does make one fact clear: submission to civil authority has limits.

So how do we know when to submit and when to rebel? One word in verse 21 gives us the key to unlock the principle. It tells us that the midwives "feared" God. They knew that Pharaoh's command to murder the male children contradicted God's moral code (Gen. 9:6), and as a result, they obeyed a law higher than Pharaoh's. By saying "no" to him, they said "yes" to God (see also Acts 4:19; 5:29).

Hard Times Don't Erase God's Promises

Though the Hebrews suffered under heavy oppression, God blessed them and increased their population. How did the Egyptians respond? With "dread" (Exod. 1:12). This term in Hebrew, *quts* (pronounced "kootz"), describes a loathing and abhorrence so strong that it causes a feeling of physical illness. When the Egyptians looked on the swelling Hebrew masses, they felt as though they were looking at a barbaric malignancy that was invading their refined and educated society. They were repulsed by and afraid of the thought of what might happen if they failed to contain the cancerous growth in their collective body.[2]

But all the abuse they strapped onto the Hebrews' backs could not crush the promise that God had made to Abraham so many years before (Gen. 15:13–14). God's program keeps moving, and His promises come true—no matter how hard life becomes.

2. See C. F. Keil and F. Delitzsch, comment on Genesis 46:28–34, in *The Pentateuch*, vol. 1 of *Biblical Commentary on the Old Testament*, trans. James Martin (Grand Rapids, Mich.: William B. Eerdmans Publishing Co., n.d.), p. 375.

Harsh Treatment Doesn't Escape God's Notice

Never think that God does not see your suffering. If we skip ahead in the story to Exodus 3, we hear God saying,

> "I have surely seen the affliction of My people who are in Egypt, and have given heed to their cry because of their taskmasters, for I am aware of their sufferings." (v. 7)

Neither the length of our suffering nor the severity of it is hidden from God's omniscient, caring eyes. He knows our pain, and He acts to comfort us.

Heavy Tests Don't Eclipse God's Concern

Remember the midwives? God honored them for remaining faithful under suffering, and He'll certainly do the same for us. But it's easy to question God's goodness when life is going badly. When hard times hit, we tend to wonder if He really cares.

The midwives, however, held onto their faith and remained true to God. They believed that heavy tests, including possible death for disobeying Pharaoh, would never eclipse God's concern.

Conclusion

Are you beginning to see the real world into which Moses was born? A vicious Pharaoh was hatching murderous plans, and God's people were quietly resisting. Like the babe born in a manger, Moses' birth marked the consummation of a promise made by God to His people. By God's design, Shiphrah and Puah refused to disobey Him and instead clung to their faith in His goodness and promises. With their help, a slave-woman named Jochebed would give birth to and preserve Israel's deliverer.

 Living Insights

Scripture shows over and over how brutality stems from fear. For example, King Saul feared David would seize his throne, so he tried to kill David. And David, after his affair with Bathsheba, had her husband killed because he feared that the sin would be exposed. The Egyptians were no exception. Fear also spawned their brutality toward the Hebrews—if the slaves revolted and left, not only would their economy collapse but the Hebrews might join their enemies.

Since the Bible so clearly demonstrates this relationship, it would be healthy for all of us to examine our lives and evaluate any animosities we have toward other people. Keep in mind that fear-induced anger, unlike the occasional outburst caused by frustration, tends to be an ongoing trend in a relationship. Take a moment to consider all the people in your life, and try to identify any bitterness you might be feeling toward them.

Spouse/dating partner _____

_____

Parents _____

_____

Siblings _____

_____

Children _____

_____

Neighbors _____

_____

Friends _____

_____

People at your church _____

_____

People from a different culture _____

_____

Others _____

_____

Now that you've examined your relationships with all the people in your life, list the ones, if any, you feel a fear-induced anger toward. Next to each name, describe your fear.

_____

_____

_____

_____

_____

_____

_____

_____

_____

_____

_____

_____

_____

You don't have to be afraid any longer. You can turn that uneasy relationship into a positive one with God's love because "there is no fear in love; but perfect love casts out fear" (1 John 4:18).

Chapter 2

Born after Midnight

Exodus 2:1–10

A special kind of lotus flower grows best in the mud. The thicker
the mire, the more beautiful the blossom. The same can be
said of Moses. Sown in the deep mud of a slave-persecuting nation,
he emerged in spite of Pharaoh's deadly decree, grew into a prince
of Egypt, and finally blossomed into the Hebrews' deliverer—all
thanks to the faith of a feeble slave woman. Let's enter his world
again and see how Moses' mother, Jochebed, planted a seed of faith
as she found the mire of slavery thickening around her.

*J*ochebed stepped uneasily into the Nile. The
night's icy grip on the sky had not yet begun to
break up under the warm rays of the coming sunrise. Her only light was some diluted moon-glow,
heavily diffused by a thick cloud cover. Muted and
silvery shards of light darted here and there along
the surface—she couldn't see where her steps were
landing. But she waded ahead with the certainty
that the riverbed among the reeds wouldn't surprise her with any steep drop-offs.

Jochebed was not an old woman, but she
walked like one now, knee-deep in the water with
her weight over her toes and each step slowly and
deliberately measured. One slip on the muddy
bottom and she and the pitch-tar basket in her
arms would fall with a loud splash, drowning the
meticulous plot she had been planning through
weeks of thought and prayer.

She glanced at the east bank. Was her daughter in the proper position? One of the puzzle pieces

in her plan was to have Miriam watch from a distance and intervene when the right time came.

Jochebed came to the thick cluster of reeds where she had decided to place the basket. The bamboo-like stalks were thick enough to hold it still against the slow, steady pull of the current and close enough to the royal bathing eddy to grab the attention of Myrrina, Pharaoh's daughter, with the soft cry of a waking baby. Hopefully, Myrrina would believe the baby to be a gift from Hapi, the Nile god, and claim him as her own. But if the package was placed too close to the bathing area, Myrrina would immediately recognize it as a contrived plan instead of a gift from Hapi. The trick was in knowing where to place the basket. Far enough to avoid suspicion, but close enough to hear the baby's cries.

If the princess responded favorably, Miriam would approach her and ask if she would like her to seek out a Hebrew woman to breast-feed the infant. If the princess agreed, Miriam would immediately get Jochebed. By God's grace, Jochebed would be deemed acceptable and granted at least a few more months with her baby.

Gently, she lowered the basket until it bobbed in the water; then she opened the lid to say her last good-bye. Her little man was growing so fast, becoming too old to hide. She caressed his cheek for what she hoped wouldn't be the last time and choked back a sob. He looked so peaceful as he slept. Such a contrast to the emotions erupting inside her. They were so close, and yet they were worlds apart. She cradled a finger in his palm, and he gently squeezed it with his tiny hand. An instinctive response to his mommy's touch.

"Would it have been easier, my child," she whispered close to his face, "if I had done this when you were born? Would I have felt less pain than I do now in giving you away? These last three months have been so precious." She had to speak as though she would never see him again. "I love you. You won't remember me, but I will never forget you. I will love you until the day I die. I pray now that Adonai intervenes and that you will continue to suckle at my breast."

The first golden ray of dawn shot through the clouds in a thin beam, but Jochebed's heart was overcast with an impending sense of loss. The princess would soon come out to the river to bathe. The baby would soon wake and begin to cry. But Miriam would be watching. The only thing left to do was wait. She tucked the blanket a little more firmly around his shoulders and bent down and kissed him on the forehead.

"Good-bye, my son," she said. Then she secured the lid and took flight for home as fast as she could, praying harder than she ever had.

Born after Midnight

Dark times often require desperate measures, don't they? As difficult as circumstances may be, however, they do provide an opportunity to exercise faith in God's deliverance and to do what pleases Him. Jochebed's attempt to save Moses shows that she chose the way of faith. Let's take a look at what happened as a result of her bold choice to trust God.

A Princess' Discovery

> The daughter of Pharaoh came down to bathe
> at the Nile,[1] with her maidens walking alongside the
> Nile; and she saw the basket among the reeds and
> sent her maid, and she brought it to her. When she
> opened it, she saw the child, and behold, the boy
> was crying. And she had pity on him and said, "This
> is one of the Hebrews' children." (Exod. 2:5–6)

The first phase of the plan worked! The princess came to the Nile as planned; maybe she heard the baby crying on cue, maybe she heard the basket scraping against the reeds or the water lapping. Whatever the reason, she compassionately rescued him. Jochebed's faith-filled preparation had paid off. Her little boy was safe from the dangers of the river and Pharaoh's decree.[2]

Does Jochebed's triumph guarantee success for us when we choose the way of faith? Scripture never promises that God will intervene—even when we plan carefully like Jochebed did. But the Bible does make it clear that God wants us to exercise faith and that faith always brings God's approval (see Heb. 11).

Jochebed's plan went far beyond saving her son from death in the Nile. Now for the second phase—the part of the plan that would determine if she would once again hold her baby in her arms.

The Suggestion

> Then his sister said to Pharaoh's daughter, "Shall I
> go and call a nurse for you from the Hebrew women
> that she may nurse the child for you?" (Exod. 2:7)

How convenient for the princess. Practically the instant her maid drew the basket from the Nile, a Hebrew servant girl came out of nowhere to help provide someone to breast-feed the baby.

---

1. Hapi, the god of the Nile, supposedly possessed the powers of nourishment and fertility. Note the irony that Pharaoh's daughter could have been seeking this god's help in having a baby, only to find a baby in the river. See Walter C. Kaiser Jr., "Exodus," in *The Expositor's Bible Commentary*, gen. ed. Frank E. Gaebelein (Grand Rapids, Mich.: Zondervan Publishing House, Academic and Professional Books, 1990), vol. 2, p. 309; "Hap, or Hapi, the God of the Nile," at http://touregypt.net/hapi.htm, part of the "Tour Egypt" web site, accessed May 1998.

2. How ironic that the very river which meant death to the Hebrew babies was the means of saving Moses! God will continually be turning evil around for His good purposes throughout Moses' story.

Pharaoh's daughter quickly told Miriam,

> "Go ahead." So the girl went and called the child's mother. (v. 8)

Can you imagine Jochebed's joy when she saw Miriam's smile as the girl ran to tell her the good news? What a blessing from God! And sometimes, God blesses us beyond what we ever imagine.

> Then Pharaoh's daughter said to her, "Take this child away and nurse him for me and I will give you your wages." So the woman took the child and nursed him. (v. 9)

Jochebed not only received her child back, but now she would receive pay for rearing him until he was at least two or even three years old.[3] The money in her hand certainly paled in comparison to the baby in her arms, but what a wonderful confirmation from God. She stepped out in faith, asking only for the life of her child, and He in turn responded with more than she ever imagined.

A New Home and a New Name

During those years of tenderly nursing and training her son, Jochebed knew she must prepare herself for the day she would have to give him up for good.

> The child grew, and she brought him to Pharaoh's daughter and he became her son. And she named him Moses, and said, "Because I drew him out of the water." (v. 10)

Can you imagine Jochebed's pain as she watched her son enter another woman's arms and be given another name? It's beyond words. But maybe she felt a deeper void when she returned to her shanty without the son who would never again be hers.[4]

In addition to a new home, Moses was given his new name. Ironically, or perhaps providentially, the one who was named because he was "drawn out" would become the one who would "draw out" the Hebrews from Egypt. In all of the pain, God was working.

---

3. "In Israel a child was not usually weaned until it was at least two, and sometimes even three. Until then it was breast-fed by its mother or sometimes by a wet-nurse." J. A. Thompson, *Handbook of Life in Bible Times* (Downers Grove, Ill.: InterVarsity Press, 1986), p. 83.

4. Jochebed's pain would be shared with Moses' father, Amram, his three-year-old brother, Aaron, and his sister Miriam (see Exod. 6:20).

He was taking someone condemned by the world—a Hebrew boy—
and turning him into a deliverer by placing him in the very palace
that had condemned him.[5]

Despite her loss, Jochebed contributed to God's plan in a significant way. She chose the way of faith and preserved the life of
Israel's deliverer. What do her actions teach us about faith?

Faith and Planning

The key to her faith lies in the fact that it was well placed and
well balanced. It was well placed because her trust was in God. It
was well balanced because, while she trusted in Him for the things
she could not control, she planned for the things she could. When
she placed that basket in the Nile, she put it in a strategic
location—in a thick cluster of reeds so it wouldn't float away, near
enough the princess to be noticed, yet far enough away to avoid
suspicion. She thought it through and came up with a plan. She
utilized Miriam to appear on the scene and make a bold suggestion.
The whole event was orchestrated, and nothing within her power
was left to chance.

Some Christians in our day have a strange concept of true faith.
They believe that if we make plans, we're taking matters into our
own hands and demonstrating a lack of trust in God. But God calls
us to have courageous faith, not reckless faith. Reckless faith is not
faith at all—it's presumption. Scripture clearly teaches us not to
put God to the test (Matt. 4:7). Therefore, people with true faith
trust God to handle the problems beyond their control and think
through the rest. In other words, wisdom doesn't contradict faith—
it complements it.

 Living Insights

Not all of us were born after midnight, but at some point, we
all pass through dark, moonless nights in our spiritual walks. Sometimes this happens in the context of relationships: a difficult friend,

---

5. Ronald Youngblood and Walter C. Kaiser Jr. additionally point out that "throughout this
early part of Exodus, all the pharaoh's efforts to suppress Israel were thwarted by women: the
midwives (1:17), the Israelite mothers (1:19), Moses' mother and sister (vv. 3–4, 7–9), the
pharaoh's daughter (here). The pharaoh's impotence to destroy the people of God is thus
ironically exposed." Note on Exodus 2:10, in *The NIV Study Bible*, gen. ed. Kenneth L.
Barker (Grand Rapids, Mich.: Zondervan Bible Publishers, 1985), p. 89.

an ugly divorce, an abusive relative. Sometimes our circumstances attempt to smother our faith: poverty, poor health, or constant moving from home to home.

Whatever the situation, we have a decision to make when those times come. We can either despair, descending into bitterness and anger, or we can respond in the Spirit, which will lead us to greater faith and effectiveness for God. Jochebed could have fallen into a depression over losing her son. She could have become angry, fought the system, and despised her situation. Instead, she responded in faith, and she *and* Moses became powerful tools in God's hand.

Has a dark midnight enveloped your life? What decision will you make? Have depression and anger already begun to take root in your heart? How can you pull those weeds from your life?

_____

_____

_____

_____

_____

If your testing hasn't yet come, now is the time to prevent bitterness from ever establishing itself. How? Through a robust faith in God. Faith will help you make a constructive response, leading you to become the most you can be for God's glory. What's the condition of your faith?

_____

_____

_____

_____

To become faith-filled believers, we must train ourselves. Just as athletes lay a foundation of physical fitness in order to perfect their game, so Christians must lay a foundation of understanding God's goodness before their faith can be perfected. Take a moment to look over the following verses, and write out what they say about God's character and how he treats His children.

Joshua 1:9 _____

_____

_____

_____

Psalm 138:7–8 _____

_____

_____

_____

Isaiah 43:2 _____

_____

_____

_____

Matthew 7:7–11 _____

_____

_____

_____

John 3:16 _____

_____

_____

_____

Now that you've had a chance to reflect on how God feels about you and what He's willing to do on your behalf, will you step out in faith and trust Him through the dark times? Remember the lotus blossom—beautiful things do come from hard times. Jochebed stepped into the Nile, and God honored her by elevating her son. She glorified God, and by faith, the same can be true of you.

Chapter 3

GOD'S WILL, MY WAY
Exodus 2:11–15; Acts 7:21–29

E asier said than done." How many times have we heard that worn-out, overused cliché? Like an old saddle that's been ridden hard and hung up wet after a thousand trail rides, we'd love to replace it but just can't find a fitting successor. Few statements, though, could be more true of Moses as he sought to fulfill God's calling on his life.

Now, many of us were taught in Sunday school that Moses didn't know God's calling until he talked with God at the burning bush, but the biblical text suggests that he knew his calling before he even left Egypt. In fact, we'll see in this chapter how Moses actively sought to become Israel's leader. We'll explore this idea more later, but now let's enter the scene as Moses spots an opportunity to start fulfilling Yahweh's calling on his life.

M oses paced down the ghetto walkway, the rough leather straps from his makeshift sandals rubbing open blisters on his supple, Egyptian-groomed heels. He was attempting to limp with the hobbled stride of a tired Hebrew, and the burn of the blisters was making his gait more realistic. He pulled his cloak further over his eyes, taking advantage of the shadowy dusk now settling over the Nile delta.

Disguised as a slave, he roamed the alleys and mud streets of Goshen—the slum district housing most of the brick makers and their families. These people were the backbone of Hebrew society. If he was going to lead this nation of slaves out of bondage, he would have to win their support.

He came to the second-to-last alley. Time and

space were running out. The sun was fading, and he needed a sign from God, anything that would give him an opportunity to demonstrate his love for these people and the desire to lead them in an uprising.

He approached the corner leading into the alley but stopped short of entering. An intermittent thudding sound came from deep within. It sounded like the soft, dull thumping a man makes when he strikes his middle finger against a fresh melon—only deeper and louder. Moses silently slipped around the edge of the corner shanty and peered into the dark corridor. His discovery of the sound's source nauseated him.

The silhouette of an Egyptian overseer stood over the shadow of a Hebrew slave on all fours. He was hunched over and holding his ribs. The whip in the overseer's hand remained coiled, but his right foot was thrusting deep into the slave's side with sickening force.

"Never, never argue with me," the overseer grunted in a muted command.

The slave's arms couldn't hold his torso's weight any longer. His elbows buckled and his chest hit the ground, forcing blood to spurt from his lips. "*Hoshi'ani, Adonai, min-hakoff re'shayim,*" he gurgled in his native tongue. "Save me, O Lord, from the hands of the wicked. Send your deliverer now, for my life is ending."

That was all Moses needed to hear. He looked down both sides of the street to make sure no other overseers were around, then he plunged into the shadows. He charged forward and sunk his fist into the overseer's kidney. The man staggered, then reeled around, his own clenched hand seeking to land a punch—the instinctive response of a war-hardened warrior. Moses ducked and missed the blow, but his cloak flew off. Their eyes met as the overseer stepped back to gather himself. He took a quick glance at his attacker, but instead of countering swiftly with a strike of his own, he took a long, second look at his assailant. He squinted—his eyes were telling him that it was Prince Moses, but his mind wasn't believing them.

With the Egyptian's weight still on his heels, Moses landed a swift, fatal blow to the nose, ending the overseer's life . . . and the slave's torment.

Moses gathered the Hebrew into his arms and carried him to a nearby shanty. He set him at the doorway, not remembering which house belonged to the midwife. He would find help for the slave first, then he would bury the evidence.

Unexpected Outcome

Having asserted his role as Israel's deliverer, Moses awoke the next morning and headed back to his people. This time to organize the leaders and begin plotting their escape. But he ran into a problem before he even made it there.

> He went out the next day, and behold, two Hebrews were fighting with each other; and he said to the offender, "Why are you striking your companion?" But he said, "Who made you a prince or a judge over us? Are you intending to kill me as you killed the Egyptian?" (Exod. 2:13–14a)

What a slap in the face! Not only was the Hebrew's retort an insult to Moses personally, but it also must have raised a question in Moses' mind. Hadn't God communicated His plan to the Israelites? Didn't they know he was their deliverer? Obviously not. This complication, as bad as it was, marked only the beginning of Moses' problems.

> Then Moses was afraid and said, "Surely the matter has become known." When Pharaoh heard of this matter, he tried to kill Moses. But Moses fled from the presence of Pharaoh and settled in the land of Midian. (vv. 14b–15a)

Can you imagine how Moses felt? He bet the whole farm in one bold throw, and the dice came up snake-eyes. He gave up his whole life—his Egyptian wealth, status, and prestige—for the sake of the Hebrews. Because they didn't know God's plan, however, they refused his leadership, and now Moses was relegated to a life of exile in a dust-coated, sun-baked wasteland. He was headed toward the edge of the earth, with no foreseeable future ahead of him.

What lesson did Moses learn from this whole ordeal? "Easier said than done." But let's not stand at a distance pitying or judging him. We, too, run the risk of making the same mistake if we don't learn from his. Let's backtrack into his past to see where he probably took a wrong turn.

Egyptian Upbringing

Moses' Egyptian upbringing certainly looked like the right preparation for becoming Israel's deliverer. When Moses was young, Pharaoh's daughter educated him according to the highest standards of the day. Acts 7:22a tells us, "Moses was educated in all the learning of the Egyptians." Most likely, he was placed under the tutelage of the world's finest teachers—the instructors at the school associated with the Temple of the Sun, which was known as "the Oxford of Ancient Egypt."[1] Alfred Edersheim notes that he would have received the best education the Egyptians had to offer.

> Education was carried to a very great length, and,

---

1. F. B. Meyer, *Great Men of the Bible* (Grand Rapids, Mich.: Zondervan Publishing House, 1981), vol. 1, p. 157.

in the case of those destined for the higher profes-
sions, embraced not only the various sciences, as
mathematics, astronomy, chemistry, medicine, etc.,
but theology, philosophy, and a knowledge of the
laws. There can be no doubt that, as the adopted
son of the princess, Moses would receive the highest
training.[2]

Moses was likely a great student, because the text itself says,
"He was a man of power in words and deeds" (v. 22b).

Moses' training definitely prepared him for military confronta-
tions. Josephus records that he led the Egyptian army in a riveting
victory over Ethiopia.[3] So Moses was a brilliant student and military
strategist, a respected warrior who was bronzed by the sun, scarred
by battle, and tempered by experience. If there was ever a leader
qualified to release Israel from slavery's chains, Moses was it.

Yet Moses still failed. God must require something more. Maybe
qualifications alone don't guarantee success. Maybe God's leaders
need to have a sensitivity to His timing as well as skill and knowledge.

Operation Self-Will

Lacking any sense of God's timing, Moses rushed into a campaign to install himself as the Hebrews' leader. Before we can examine this campaign, however, we need to understand how he came
to know God's calling, because some of us may still be wondering,
"How did Moses know God's plan before the burning bush?"

God's Calling

Scripture tells us that Moses decided "to visit his brethren, the
sons of Israel," when he was about forty years old (Acts 7:23; see
also Exod. 2:11). Granted, Moses could have considered the Hebrews his "brethren" without thinking of himself as their deliverer,
but his "visit" to them raises an interesting question. With more
than two million Hebrews residing near Goshen at the time,
couldn't Moses have seen them anytime he wanted? Of course he

2. Alfred Edersheim, *Bible History: Old Testament* (reprint, Grand Rapids, Mich.: William B.
Eerdmans Publishing Co., 1987), p. 39.

3. Flavius Josephus, *Antiquities of the Jews*, book 2, chapter 10, in *The Works of Flavius Josephus*,
trans. William Whiston, from the Internet site http:.//wesley.nnc.edu/josephus/, accessed May
1998.

could have. Therefore, this visit must be seen as more than just an attempt to "hang out" with his own kind. It was a special visit with an important purpose—to build a relationship with the people he would save.

In addition, Moses demonstrated knowledge of God's plan by trying to establish his leadership among the Hebrews through unifying them.

> "On the following day he appeared to them as they were fighting together, and he tried to reconcile them in peace, saying, 'Men, you are brethren, why do you injure one another?'" (Acts 7:26)

And his motivation for doing so is revealed in verse 25: "And he supposed that his brethren understood that God was granting them deliverance through him, but they did not understand." One fact is clear from these verses: Moses knew he was supposed to be Israel's leader long before he left Egypt.

Moses' Way

Now, did God call Moses to kill the Egyptian? The Bible never records God's saying so. Instead, Exodus 2:12 says Moses "looked this way and that"—but never up to God. He didn't wait for God's explicit command or His protection. Moses simply saw an opportunity and seized it. As a result, he failed to accomplish God's will and brought suffering on himself.

Painful Consequences

Moses reaped a bountiful harvest of confusion and frustration by sowing the seeds of self-will. Can you imagine the puzzled look on his face as the two Hebrew men told him to keep his nose out of their business (v. 14; Acts 7:27-28)? He was the peacemaker, after all, their unifier. They should have been grateful for his guidance and eager for his leadership! Maybe Moses thought his murdering the overseer would catalyze the slaves to rally around him. Instead, it became an insult and indictment to him.

The seeds of self-will also produced a host of unbearable conditions. When Moses realized the overseer's murder would become a card played against him, his hope turned to fear (Exod. 2:14), with good reason. When Pharaoh heard about the killing, he put a price on Moses' head (v. 15a).

So Moses ran.

Moses fled from the presence of Pharaoh and settled
in the land of Midian, and he sat down by a well.
(v. 15b)

Culmination: Discouragement and Defeat

"Operation Self-Will" led Moses into a desert experience of
discouragement and defeat. His journey teaches us two principles
about trying to fulfill God's will our own way. First, we learn that
when the self-life runs its course, it settles in a desert. It seems most of
us simply refuse to stop until God causes everything to dry up.
Often, we keep barging ahead until we end up nowhere. And second, we learn that *when the self-life finally sits down, the well of a new
life is near.* God's purpose is not to abandon us in the desert but help
us come to the end of ourselves so that we can be filled with Him.
F. B. Meyer illuminates this for us.

> Moses was out of touch with God. So he fled, and
> crossed the desert that lay between him and the
> eastern frontier; threaded the mountain passes of the
> Sinaitic peninsula, through which in after years he
> was to lead his people; and at last sat wearily down
> by a well in the land of Midian. . . .
>
> Such experiences come to us all. We rush for-
> ward, thinking to carry all before us; we strike a few
> blows in vain; we are staggered with disappointment,
> and reel back; . . . we flee from the scenes of our
> discomfiture to hide ourselves in chagrin. Then we
> are hidden in the secret of God's presence from the
> pride of man. And there our vision clears: the
> silt drops from the current of our life, . . . our self-
> life dies down; our spirits drink of the river of God,
> . . . our faith begins to grasp his arm, . . . and
> thus at last we emerge to be his hand to lead an
> Exodus.[4]

"Easier said than done." That sums it up when we try to do
God's will our own way. But fulfilling His calling was never meant
to be so difficult. We can become successful doers of His will, and

---

4. F. B. Meyer, *Moses: The Servant of God* (Grand Rapids, Mich.: Zondervan Publishing
House, 1953), pp. 31–32.

minimize our desert times, when we use wisdom—by realizing not only that we need to know His will, but we must also pursue it His way.

 Living Insights

How are you doing with detecting and following God's will? Are you in the center of it and reaping a rich harvest of His blessings? Praise God for that. Maybe, though, you're a little more like Moses.

Perhaps you're a "type A" personality, and you're trying to initiate or accomplish your calling your own way. You may be highly qualified and gifted, and some opportunities have surfaced. But instead of consulting the Lord, you've tackled them immediately, and now things aren't moving as quickly or strongly as you'd hoped. If this describes your situation, take a minute to reflect on this principle: *When the self-life runs its course, it settles in a desert.* Are you willing to stop where you are and seek God's direction, before you wind up in the desert?

_____

_____

Have the consequences of your actions progressed beyond confusion to pain? Are you in the middle of the desert, with parched sand and hot sun as far as your eye can see? Maybe your energy and zeal have long since shriveled up under the heat of unmet expectations, and you're beginning to wonder if God will ever use you. If so, remember this principle: *When the self-life sits down, the well of a new life is near.* Take a moment to let Moses' story encourage you. God's well is near. His refreshment is provided for you. Write out a prayer to the Lord, and let Him lead you to a renewed strength and a refocused vision.

_____

_____

_____

_____

Chapter 4

LESSONS LEARNED FROM FAILURE

Exodus 2:11–25

O f all the emotions Moses may have felt as a result of fleeing into exile, bitterness and confusion would probably have been at the top of the list. Why hadn't God told the Hebrews about His plan? Why would He tell Moses and not the others? Humanly speaking, Moses could have made a strong argument for blaming God for the whole mess. Did he? Or did he accept the truth that he was the one who failed and learn from it?

Looking Back: Learning from Failure

What can we learn from failure? With the right attitude, we can experience a dynamic transformation in our ways of thinking. Our mistakes can provide an opportunity for a new beginning. But we must choose to consider failure not as a taskmaster but as a teacher. Moses' situation reveals four principles that can help us turn our failures into opportunities.

Spiritual Ends Are Not Achieved by Carnal Means

Remember when Moses "struck down the Egyptian and hid him in the sand" (Exod. 2:12b)? He acted on his own, without any directive from God. As a consequence, he ended up as a desert nomad instead of a national leader. No one ever sows a carnal seed and reaps a spiritual fruit. It is preposterous to manipulate, connive, scheme, and lie at all, even more so when you're trying to accomplish God's will. Moses' flesh-driven plan could never have produced a godly end.

Timing Is as Important as Action

God not only wants us to follow Him, He wants us to follow at His pace. Moses prematurely tried to push his way into leadership rather than wait on the Lord to move him into that position. As a result, no one followed him (vv. 13–14). When God is in a plan, it flows; when the flesh is in it, it's forced. Moses learned that waiting on God is the mark of wisdom and strength, not foolishness and weakness.

Hiding the Wrong Done Does Not Erase It

When Moses tried to hide his murderous act by burying the Egyptian overseer in the sand (v. 12b), he exercised a sinful muscle that had been in the human race since Adam and Eve. After the two ate from the forbidden tree, they tried to cover up their sin by clothing themselves with fig leaves and hiding from God (Gen. 3:1–8). The cover-up failed, and divine judgment followed (vv. 9–19). For us, too, attempts to conceal sin only delay its discovery and intensify the severity of the failure.

Spiritual Leadership Is God-Appointed, Not Self-Assumed

Moses had an incredible résumé. He was raised in the right neighborhood, schooled in the best institution, respected as a powerful speaker and leader, recognized as a man of principle, and to top it all off, he was physically attractive (Exod. 2:2; Acts 7:20–22; Heb. 11:23–26). But simply because he had been groomed for national leadership in Egypt did not mean that he was ready to take the reins of spiritual leadership for Israel. None of us can adequately lead God's people until we become His consistent followers. Moses, consciously or not, tried to take God's place rather than obediently follow His lead.

Did Moses learn these lessons? Let's catch up with him as he arrives in Midian and see if he was willing to grow from his mistakes.

Moses eased his aching body down by the base of the well. He didn't know the name of the nearby village, but he was fairly sure he had made it into Midian. He dropped his fringed cloak, which he used as a bag to hold his water flasks and raisins. The load plopped to the ground, aggravating small corkscrews of dust from their slumber on the desert floor. *So much for that thing,* Moses thought, as he poked a finger into the intricately embroidered

Egyptian linen cloak, now soiled and stained beyond repair.

He leaned back against the well and watched as a vagrant wind chased clouds of dust back and forth across the valley basin. The breeze on his face soothed him a little, but the lumpy surface of the well jabbed his back in several places. He didn't move—he was too tired, even to fidget. . . . Then the foul stench of a sea of goats wafted over him.

He rose and dusted himself off just as a clamorous herd began trickling from the steep mountain trail and onto the well's flat watering ground. Wave after wave of thirsty sheep and goats crowded the area, pushing Moses back into a crevice between two boulders. As he watched from the crevice, seven young women waded through the wool, dust, and stench to the water. One began drawing buckets from the well and passing them to the others, who dumped the contents into troughs on the fringe of the area. From the pattern and color of the women's clothing, Moses knew he was in Midian for sure.

"Well, well, well," a low, gravely voice bellowed from the bluff above. "Look who's come to water their flock, boys!" Moses could almost smell the shepherd's stench over the sheep's.

"Out of the way, Zipporah," the shepherd said, "you and your flock. We've spent half the day driving our sheep to this well. We're not about to give it up to a bunch of women."

The shepherd signaled to his companions, and they began driving back the women's sheep. "I do want to thank you for pouring our water," he sneered. "Your daddy has raised such considerate servant girls."

The women protested, but their sheep were fleeing the shepherds' rods. In only moments, their whole flock would be scattered so that the other herd could move in. With his walking staff clenched in his right fist, Moses leapt from the crevice. The strong wouldn't get the best of the weak this time, not if he could help it.

◆

Jethro[1] heard the excited voices of his daughters and hurried out of the tent. It was barely past midday, and they were supposed to be out with the sheep. He stepped into the middle of the encampment, but the women were so preoccupied with reliving Moses' rescue that they nearly walked right into their father.

"Stop!" Jethro shouted. The women came to an abrupt halt, trying to obey him while struggling to contain their excitement. "What are you doing home so early?"

Zipporah answered, "The most amazing thing happened, Father. Barak's shepherds tried to steal our water again, but then this man showed up. I think he's Egyptian—his clothes looked a little bit like the traders' and his accent sounded that way. But he jumped out from the rocks and defended

---

1. The "priest of Midian" is called Reuel, which means "friend of God," in 2:18, and Jethro, possibly meaning "His excellency" or "His abundance," in 3:1. Why two different names? No one knows for sure, but it's possible that Reuel was a family or clan name and Jethro might have been a title.

us. This Egyptian not only drove the men away but watered our sheep!"

"Where is this man?" Jethro asked. "Go get him so we can feed him and welcome him into our home for the night."

They gladly hurried off—this was exactly what they had wanted to hear from their father.

When they returned with Moses, both men sensed a mutual respect for each other. Moses took a permanent place in Jethro's household, accepted Zipporah in marriage, and welcomed his first son, Gershom.[2]

Looking Ahead: Responding to Failure

Moses' actions in Midian demonstrate that he did learn the lessons failure can teach, and that his heart changed just as much as his mind did. Lessons are helpful, but head knowledge is not enough to make a real difference in someone's walk with God. That knowledge must soak into a person's heart and deeds. Let's consider three important changes that Moses experienced as a result of his internal transformation. These changes should also characterize our lives as we seek to serve the Lord.

The Development of a Servant's Attitude

What did Moses do when the seven women were harassed at the well?

> Now the priest at Midian had seven daughters; and they came to draw water and filled the troughs to water their father's flock. Then the shepherds came and drove them away, but Moses stood up and helped them and watered their flock. (Exod. 2:16–17)

---

2. Gershom most likely means "an alien there," because Moses was an alien in a foreign land.

Moses not only defended the women, which would have been the chivalrous response for any man in any age, but he also watered the livestock—hardly the role of a Pharaoh-elect of Egypt. Moses stepped among those smelly sheep and helped the women with their work. Failure was cultivating a servant's attitude in him.

The Willingness to Be Obscure

Moses, an Egyptian prince, accepted an invitation to become a member of a shepherd's clan. This once-promising ruler was submitting himself to a priest who served a group of nomadic shepherds:

> When [the women] came to Reuel their father, he said, "Why have you come back so soon today?" So they said, "An Egyptian delivered us from the hand of the shepherds, and what is more, he even drew the water for us and watered the flock." He said to his daughters, "Where is he then? Why is it that you have left the man behind? Invite him to have something to eat." Moses was willing to dwell with the man, and he gave his daughter Zipporah to Moses. Then she gave birth to a son, and he named him Gershom, for he said, "I have been a sojourner in a foreign land." (vv. 18–22; see also 3:1)

By marrying Zipporah and starting a family, Moses showed his willingness to step away from the world's most powerful throne and toil in the shadows of an obscure home in a barren land.

The Ability to Rest and Rely on God

The final verses of Exodus 2 paint a bleak and tragic scene with God as the single ray of hope.

> Now it came about in the course of those many days that the king of Egypt died. And the sons of Israel sighed because of the bondage, and they cried out; and their cry for help because of their bondage rose up to God. So God heard their groaning; and God remembered His covenant with Abraham, Isaac, and Jacob. God saw the sons of Israel, and God took notice of them. (2:23–25)

Did you notice that no mention is made of Moses? Although he probably continued receiving reports of the Hebrews' misery from the caravans passing through Midian, he did not run back and initiate another premature attempt to free them. Instead, he spent forty years raising a family and pasturing a flock, while trusting God to deliver the Hebrews in His own way and in His own time. Moses had definitely had a change of heart.

Christians, and especially those who want to become spiritual leaders, must hold these truths in both their minds and hearts, displaying them in their words and actions. If we remember and practice these principles, our failures won't be the last word but only the start of a more mature life.

Concluding Thoughts about Failure

People usually make mistakes over and over again because they don't stop to learn from them. The more times we fail to learn from a mistake, the more severe the consequences can be. Frustration over this vicious cycle can drive us into a wilderness experience that drains our strength, dries up our confidence, and blurs our ministry vision. It's unfortunate that God must often lead us into the desert before we will listen to and heed His Word. But the good news is that we do not have to die of thirst.

We can use our failures to move closer to God's well of renewed vision and empowerment. Facing failure honestly, coming to the end of ourselves, and turning to God not only promotes an obedient life, it also prompts a teachable spirit (compare the similar effect of affliction in Ps. 119:67, 71). However, if we keep running down the same flesh-driven paths, then our feelings of despair, loneliness, and uselessness will only increase; and our walk with God will continue to suffer. The alternatives are clear. And the choice between them is ours.

Which option will you choose today?

 Living Insights

Moses turned his failure into a victory. Even before he led the Hebrews through the Red Sea, he experienced a triumph within himself by learning from his mistakes. When we learn from our shortcomings, we take pressure off ourselves and make room for

God to work through us. Use the following scales to evaluate your-self (1 is nonexistent, 10 is consistent success).

My attitude as a servant:

1 2 3 4 5 6 7 8 9 10

My willingness to be obscure:

1 2 3 4 5 6 7 8 9 10

My ability to rest and rely on God:

1 2 3 4 5 6 7 8 9 10

How did you do? Wrap up this chapter by crafting a prayer to God, explaining to Him some of the ministry goals you're currently pursuing. If you are experiencing His blessing and abundance, there's no need to question if He's behind it or not. But if you've run into a wall or two, ask Him to help you examine your motives. You may need to make a few adjustments.

_____

_____

_____

_____

_____

_____

_____

_____

_____

_____

_____

_____

_____

Chapter 5

THE DESERT: SCHOOL OF SELF-DISCOVERY

Exodus 2:21–22; 3:1

Moses wiped the sweat from his eyebrow and squinted into the distance. With the sun already setting behind Mount Horeb,[1] faraway objects became nebulous in the purple haze of dusk. He couldn't tell if he was looking at a faraway caravan kicking up a cloud or just a rock jutting from the sand.

"You better get going," he said to the Egyptian trader, who had stopped to sell his goods and to talk, it seemed, until his lips were chapped. "It looks like another caravan's making its way to the coast."

"Very well," the trader said. "You don't want to buy anything; I fully understand. But what if I offered a simple exchange?"

"No. I'm not interested." Moses was beginning to wonder if this trader was dense or if he was ignoring the hints for some other reason.

"A question, then."

Here it came. Moses knew there had to be something else.

"You are Midianite, and yet your name—it's Egyptian. I'm old, so I remember that an Egyptian prince by that same name disappeared many years ago. The young men don't know. In fact, they don't

---

1. Mount Horeb is another name for Mount Sinai.

know anything these days. The schools have gone down so much since I was young. As a matter of fact, when I was twelve . . ."

"No," Moses interrupted.

"No, what?" the trader asked.

"No, I'm not named after the prince of Egypt, nor am I related to him."

"No, I imagine you wouldn't be. After all, a pharaoh would never allow a relative of his to work as a lowly shepherd in Midian."

The trader spurred his camel into motion and headed down the trail toward the Sinai region.

Moses thought about what the trader had said. "A shepherd," he whispered to himself. "What an existence. And I could be leading a nation."

The School of Self-Discovery

The trader was right. In the world's eyes, Moses was a fool, and maybe even he felt like one. He had learned many skills and disciplines in Egypt, and apparently he was throwing all that training away on a flock of sheep. But Moses' upbringing in Egypt was only half of what he needed to fulfill God's calling. His character still needed refining. So God sent him to graduate school in the desert.

There he learned to lead and nurture a stinky herd of sheep and goats—a seemingly futile occupation for a man wanting to deliver a nation. Maybe Moses became convinced that his chance had passed. Forty years of shepherding in the desert would be enough to cause even the most driven man to question his future. But God still had a plan for him, and little did he realize how much those smelly sheep would teach him about leading an ungrateful and fickle people to their Promised Land.

God's Use of the Desert

Before we join Moses in his desert, let's bring the heat a little closer to home. Have you ever felt set aside, unproductive, helpless in the backlash of painful circumstances? You may very well be going through a desert. How can you survive? The book of Deuteronomy presents two important truths about the desert that we need to understand for the experience to make us rather than break us.

God Is with Us in the Desert

First, God uses the desert to teach us to appreciate His presence. The desert does this by stripping away everything else we rely on for strength and security. It's a desolate place with no comforting signs of life—only the biting sand, howling wind, and waves of heat. Deuteronomy 32:10 pictures the desert as a "howling waste of a wilderness." Naturally, then, we respond in fear. We might feel like God's gone, that we're all alone, that we'll never survive.

But God is never gone, and all believers will make it through their desert experiences if they learn to rely on Him. Like a person recovering from a broken leg, every one of us must learn to trust again by walking without crutches. In the desert, God removes those crutches and replaces them with an assurance of His presence. The second half of verse 10 shows how God cared for Israel in the wilderness.

> "He encircled him [Jacob/Israel], He cared for him,
> He guarded him as the pupil of His eye."

Did you catch how meticulously God cared for them? He protected them as a person protects the pupil of the eye. One of the most protected parts of the body is the eye. When the wind blows, we cover it; and when the sun glares, we shade it. God doesn't just treat us like a precious eye but like the most important part of the eye—the pupil. Even in the desert, in a place where we feel exposed and vulnerable, God protects us with the greatest of care. He encircles us, cares for us, guards us, and guides us (v. 12).

God Reveals Our Hearts in the Desert

God also uses the desert to reveal our hearts. Deuteronomy 8:2 shows that He reshapes us in the desert by humbling us, testing us, and disclosing the content of our character.

> "You shall remember all the way which the Lord

your God has led you in the wilderness these forty years, that He might humble you, testing you, to know what was in your heart, whether you would keep His commandments or not."

There's nothing like the desert for burning away false pretenses and peeling off masks. It reveals a person's strengths and weaknesses. The most secure, humble, gracious, and honest Christians are those who have been through the fire of testing and reshaped in God's mold. It takes a desert to do that.

Are you ready to see how these truths revealed themselves in Moses' life? Then let's join him in the hot, desolate expanse of Midian.

Moses' Time in the Desert

God squeezed every ounce of benefit from Moses' time in Midian. From his location to his job to the lessons he learned, God used every possible facet of Moses' life to equip him for his calling.

His Location

As we have seen, Moses lived with his father-in-law, who was "the priest of Midian" (Exod. 2:15–16, 21). Where exactly is Midian? Most maps show it bordering the eastern side of the Gulf of Aqaba, in what is now the northwest region of Saudi Arabia. But some scholars believe, based on the biblical record, that the territory may have ranged beyond northwest Arabia to encompass "southern Transjordan, the Arabah, portions of the Negeb, and possibly northern Sinai."[2]

In addition, Exodus 3:1 tells us that Moses led Jethro's flock to the "west side of the wilderness." "West side," literally, is "rear part," since the east was the direction by which everything else was judged. In other words, Moses lived in view of Mount Horeb, the mountain of God in the Sinai region. Sounds picturesque, doesn't it? Actually, it was anything but beautiful or majestic. There are only two things to look at in the Sinai—sand and rocks. No plant life, no lakes or rivers. As a result, it's a lonely place, a place where time stands still and where God began to stretch and strengthen Moses in ways he never imagined.

2. Thomas V. Brisco, "Midian, Midianites," in *The International Standard Bible Encyclopedia*, rev. ed., gen. ed. Geoffrey W. Bromiley (1986; reprint, Grand Rapids, Mich.: William B. Eerdmans Publishing Co., 1987), vol. 3, p. 350.

His Vocation

Moses' job wasn't any better than his location. Actually, he filled three roles: he was a husband to Zipporah, he was father to two sons (Exod. 18:3–4; Acts 7:29), and, of course, he was a shepherd. All three of these jobs are noble pursuits, and Scripture certainly extols the value of being a good husband, father, and worker. But a man who had set his sights on leading a nation would certainly feel frustrated when limited to just those three roles.

Through these roles, though, God once again trained Moses in unexpected ways. He learned to be patient and to share his life through the day-in, day-out work of herding sheep and supplying the needs of his wife and children.

His Education

Moses came into contact with four powerful teachers as a result of his location and vocation. Through these distinguished instructors, Moses undertook the core curriculum of the transformation of the soul and earned a degree in Self-Discovery. Let's meet each of these teachers and examine what Moses learned from them.

- *Professor Obscurity.* What a class to start off with! Moses came from a life in which he was heralded everywhere he went. As a prince, he was on his way to becoming a pharaoh, and pharaohs were considered deities. In his former life, crowds as far as the eye could see sang his praises with exalted choruses. Now he was surrounded by bleating sheep and moaning winds. In Egypt, the most brilliant minds sat at his feet. Now he herded farm animals that required a rod over their back before they would even heed his commands.

- *Professor Time.* Not only did the school of Self-Discovery start tough, it also ended tough—forty years later! Moses started his desert studies when he was forty years old and graduated at the age of eighty. Many, many times he must have wondered if he'd ever see the light at the end of the tunnel.

- *Professor Solitude.* This teacher was Moses' most important mentor. In time, Moses' own people, the Hebrews, would mount a mutiny against him. How did he cope with the pain and stress of it all? How did he stand alone against world leaders and angry mobs? He was able to do it because he had been standing alone for forty years. He had learned to not be dependent on the affirmation of others.

- *Professor Discomfort.* Moses had been through all the discomforts the desert could hand out, especially the lack of water and food. His skin was calloused, and his nerve endings were tempered. Like a veteran wilderness guide, Moses knew the pains so well that, later on, he would hardly notice them as he led his people out of Egypt and into the desert.

Our Response to the Desert

How do we typically respond to God when He leads us into a desert experience? There are three possibilities, but only one will lead us to a higher level of maturity.

"I Don't Need It"

Usually, fear or pride is at the root of a response like this, showing that we failed the classes taught by Professors Obscurity or Time. Unfortunately, when we fail, we usually have to take the class again.

"I'm Tired of It"

This response signals that we performed poorly in either Dr. Solitude's or Dr. Discomfort's class. Although our response is natural and understandable, it's usually more conducive to self-pity than self-discovery. If class has not been dismissed, if we're still in the desert, there's more to learn.

"I Accept It"

This attitude is the only one that leads to graduation and successful job placement. If you're in a desert experience, whether it be physical, emotional, or spiritual, don't try to fight it or run from it. Settle into a pattern of self-discovery and allow God to teach you about the areas in which you need to mature. No matter how useless your circumstances may seem, turn your situation over to Him and watch as He recasts your character into His mold.

Living Insights

Set aside, hidden, humbled, led to a barren land. Many of us can identify with Moses' school in the desert. But have we understood what God was doing for us there? Have we gained any insight into the way God prepares us for a deeper relationship with Him and further service for Him? Perhaps if we were to see it in black and white, it would make more sense.

Here's an idea of what God's training method looks like. Keep in mind that each line represents a barrier of resistance to God's instruction, and each space shows a stage of development through which God wants to take us, once the barrier is broken.

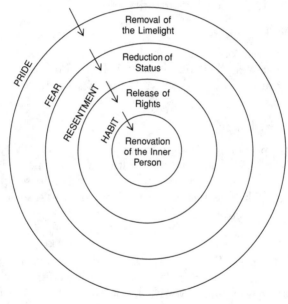

Before God can accustom us to the Light of the World, He must first remove the artificial limelight that pride shines in our eyes.

Before God can bring us to the nourishing pastures of humility, He must first take down the cardboard backdrop of status that our fears prop up.

Before God can hand us the things He would give us freely, He must first pry loose our grip on the rights our resentments hold fast.

And before God can enlarge our hearts, He must first renew our inner person by knocking loose the habits that constrict and block the flow of life.

Where are you in God's training program? Is there a certain barrier you are struggling with? What has this been like for you?

_____

_____

_____

_____

_____

_____

Which stage of development are you in the midst of? What are some of the lessons God has taught you here?

_____

_____

_____

_____

_____

_____

Though often challenging and sometimes painful, God's training method always has a purpose. Remember, it would change Moses from being a forgotten prince of Egypt to being Israel's enduring liberator and lawgiver.[3]

---

3. This Living Insight has been adapted from the study guide *The Life and Times of Elijah*, coauthored by David Lien, from the Bible-teaching ministry of Charles R. Swindoll (Anaheim, Calif.: Insight for Living, 1992), pp. 17–18.

Chapter 6

BURNING BUSHES AND SECOND CHANCES

Exodus 3:1–10

Moses drove the sheep up along the north ridge trail toward the highest pasture. The midafternoon sun started to cast long shadows, and Moses needed a break. He corralled the sheep against a bluff, unfurled his cloak like a blanket, and sat on the ground. Leaning back on his elbows, he relished the relief of resting his hard-worked muscles.

Then a glimmer caught his eye, about a hundred paces up the mountain. Something on fire. Desert bushes were known to occasionally ignite spontaneously; Moses had seen it maybe a dozen times in his forty years in Midian. Still, this one seemed unique. It burned and burned, without dying down. Curious, Moses scrambled quickly up the slope. What was causing this phenomenon?

The bush, amazingly, didn't burn out. But even more astonishing than that was the voice which spoke to Moses from it. Let's join him on the mountain and see what we can learn from this incredible encounter.

The Day

This day had been like any other for Moses—driving the sheep, pasturing them, and taking an occasional break. The opening verse of Exodus 3 emphasizes the routineness.

> Now Moses was pasturing the flock of Jethro his
> father-in-law, the priest of Midian. (v. 1a)

The text gives no indication something unique was about to happen. Rather, it was just a vanilla-flavored day wrapped in plain brown paper.

God's method is the same today. When He speaks, He usually calls us in the midst of ordinary circumstances, not in loud thunderclaps and bright flashes of lightning. His unique visits, though, still come. And such was the case with Moses.

The Bush

Moses walked beside his flock, shaking the sand from his sandals from time to time while trying to keep the sheep from wandering away and getting snagged in briar patches, occasionally sitting down to rest. Then, all of a sudden, something remarkable occurred.

> He looked, and behold, the bush was burning with
> fire, yet the bush was not consumed. So Moses said,
> "I must turn aside now and see this marvelous sight,
> why the bush is not burned up." (vv. 2b–3)

Was this some sort of supernatural bush? No—it was one of a vast number of brambles that dotted the desert landscape. How God used it, however, was what was special. It burned with His very presence (v. 2a). What does this common bush that was used in a special way reveal about how God speaks to us today?

God sometimes uses the commonplace in uncommon ways. They're much more than mere chance events—they're God's way of tapping us on the shoulder so that we'll sit up and listen to what He has to say. As Walter Kaiser Jr. notes,

> God chose the small and the despised burning bush
> as his medium of revelation, and he waited to see
> how sensitive Moses was toward the insignificant
> and small things of life before he invested him with
> larger tasks.[1]

Although we shouldn't expect God to speak to us in blazing

---

1. Walter C. Kaiser Jr., "Exodus," in *The Expositor's Bible Commentary*, gen. ed. Frank E. Gaebelein (Grand Rapids, Mich.: Zondervan Publishing House, Academic and Professional Books, 1990), vol. 2, p. 315.

bushes, lightning, and thunder, we should still listen for His voice in seemingly common things.

The Need

Not until Moses turned to look at the burning bush did God call his name (v. 4a). Keep in mind that at this point Moses probably didn't know that the voice belonged to God. All he saw was a bush on fire, with an unfamiliar and authoritative voice coming from it. He responded to the call with a simple answer, "Here I am" (v. 4b). His words indicated more than just an acknowledgment of the call; they also showed his availability to respond further. That's when God spoke to him again.

> "Do not come near here; remove your sandals from
> your feet, for the place on which you are standing
> is holy ground." (v. 5)

God commanded Moses to consider the ground sacred. He didn't mean that it was morally pure, but that it took on special significance because He was speaking to Moses on it. God's supernatural presence gave the ordinary surroundings extraordinary status. Interestingly, this is the first use of the word *holy* in all of Scripture.

Moses, out of reverence, did as he was told and removed his sandals. The Lord then followed His command with a declaration of His identity.

> "I am the God of your father, the God of Abraham,
> the God of Isaac, and the God of Jacob." (v. 6a)

When Moses heard this, he must have realized that the One he failed in Egypt was speaking to him. The text says that Moses "hid his face, for he was afraid to look at God" (v. 6b). But God kept communicating to him, telling Moses that He heard the cries of His oppressed people in Egypt and was concerned for them.

> "I have surely seen the affliction of My people who
> are in Egypt, and have given heed to their cry be-
> cause of their taskmasters, for I am aware of their
> sufferings. So I have come down to deliver them
> from the power of the Egyptians, and to bring them
> up from that land to a good and spacious land, to a
> land flowing with milk and honey, to the place of
> the Canaanite and the Hittite and the Amorite and

the Perizzite and the Hivite and the Jebusite. Now, behold, the cry of the sons of Israel has come to Me; furthermore, I have seen the oppression with which the Egyptians are oppressing them." (vv. 7–9)

At last! After his failure, Moses must have wondered if he had doomed Israel to slavery and oppression forever. What joy he must have felt to know that God had never stopped caring and would act on the Hebrews' behalf. *But why is God telling me this?* Moses might have thought.

The Call

He got his answer in the Lord's next words.

"Therefore, come now, and I will send you to Pharaoh, so that you may bring My people, the sons of Israel, out of Egypt." (v. 10)

After spending forty years in Midianite obscurity, Moses finally received God's commission to return to Egypt and deliver his people.

Responding to God's Call

What an opportunity for Moses! What a chance to start again and redeem himself as God's servant. Isn't it encouraging to think that God keeps giving us opportunities even after we've made mistakes? Even after we've failed God and think that we're useless, He still returns to restore us and call us back into service.

When He does call us, though, we need to make sure we respond in the right way. Every time God calls, we have the option to respond in one of four ways. We can run ahead before we are sent. We can retreat after we've failed. We can resist the calling. Or we can choose to remain available and respond obediently when the call comes.

Only this fourth option is the right one. It's the response of a spiritually mature believer, and it's the one God is looking for from each of us. Which one will you choose when God calls your name?

Living Insights

A nineteenth-century proverb declares, "The bird with a broken pinion [wing] Never soars as high again."[2] Sad, isn't it? But is it true? Moses' experience in Exodus 3:1–10, fortunately, shows this saying to be absolutely false—at least in relation to God's children.

Look at the list of people God mentions when He identifies Himself to Moses (v. 6): Abraham, Isaac, and Jacob. If Moses knew the truth about those guys, and he likely did, he must have felt a lot better about his own mistakes. After all, Abraham tried to jump-start God's plan by conceiving a baby with Hagar when his wife Sarai seemingly couldn't do the job. Isaac also faltered, by lying about Rebekah in the same way Abraham once lied about Sarah. And Jacob seized his father's birthright and blessing without waiting for God's help. God doesn't shy away from people with broken wings; second chances abound for the man or woman who wants to serve Him faithfully.

In what ways have you failed God in the past?

_____

_____

_____

_____

_____

_____

Do you feel disqualified from having a second chance? Why?

_____

_____

_____

_____

2. Hezekiah Butterworth, "The Bird with a Broken Wing," in *The World's Best-Loved Poems*, comp. James Gilchrist Lawson (New York, N.Y.: Harper and Row, Publishers, 1955), p. 54.

_____

_____

_____

God is so much more forgiving of us than we are of ourselves. He's a God of second chances. Claim the grace and forgiveness He offers to all who repent, won't you? Spend some time in prayer—you may even want to write your thoughts down—asking God to free you from the prison of your unforgiveness so you can serve Him with joy in all that He calls you to.

_____

_____

_____

_____

_____

_____

_____

_____

_____

_____

_____

Chapter 7

WHO ME, LORD?

Exodus 3:10–4:17

In the previous chapter, we learned that we tend to respond to God's instructions in three negative ways: we run ahead before He sends us, we retreat after we've failed, or we resist when we're called. Up to this point in Moses' life, we've seen him respond in the first two ways—he ran ahead of God by trying to take a leadership position among the Hebrews before he was told to; then, he retreated to Midian when the attempt failed. Now we're going to watch him resist when God finally calls.

Why would Moses, after all those years, resist God's call? Because during his forty-year sojourn in the desert, he over-learned his lessons in humility. By the time God spoke to him through the burning bush, he felt so inferior and incompetent that when God called him to deliver Israel out of Egypt, he replied with excuses.

Have you ever felt like Moses when God called you to a task? In this chapter, we're going to analyze each of Moses' excuses and watch how God responds. Through their dialogue, we'll be comforted by the way God promises to provide for us, and we'll learn how we can respond obediently to Him instead of resisting His call.

Moses stood before the blazing bush. It rumbled, bellowing smoke into the air that looked like gathering thunderclouds. The bramble stood higher than a grown man, and its thick foliage crackled and popped in flames that licked the air. He listened as Yahweh spoke.

"When you've revealed My plan to My people," He said, "they'll listen to you and believe that I sent you. Then you and the elders will go to Pharaoh and request permission for a three-day journey to make a sacrifice to Me, but he won't listen. So I'll visit

Egypt with so much catastrophe that they'll not only let you go, they'll give you everything they own."

When God finished speaking, Moses remembered the time he tried to keep the two slaves from fighting each other. They clearly didn't want his help, and their rebuff still stung. What a nation of mule-headed beasts the Hebrews were! Yet God spoke as though they'd go right along with everything Moses said. *What will be different this time?* Moses thought. *It sounds like the exact same thing I tried to do forty years ago!*

"What if they don't listen to me—don't believe me?" Moses asked. "What if they don't believe You appeared to me? They might say, 'God hasn't appeared to you, old man. Go back to Midian, or better yet, jump in here and help us make some bricks.' Then they'll laugh at me."

"What do you have in your hand?" God asked.

"A walking staff."

"Throw it to the ground."

Moses threw it down, and as soon as it hit the dirt, it coiled into the tight spiral of a long, black adder. Moses looked into the two dark, hollow beads staring back at him. Its eyes were like coal. There was life behind them, but no warmth; just a cold, single-minded evil.

The adder spat and hissed as Moses leapt for a nearby rock and hid in a cleft.

"Pick it up," God said, "by the tail."

The tail? Moses watched the serpent from behind the rock. It didn't look like it wanted to be picked up by any part, let alone the most dangerous.

51

He timidly stretched his hand toward the viper's tail, clenching his fist around some flesh. If the snake was going to kill him, it would do it now. But instead it fell limp on the ground and straightened back into a staff. Moses fell to his knees, his muscles quivering from the brush with death.

"Now, Moses," God said, "put your hand in your cloak . . ."

God Calls Moses

Moses had been living in exile for forty years—a long time to live in the shadow of failure. Then, without any warning, the Lord spoke, uttering the hardest words for Moses to hear.

> "Now, behold, the cry of the sons of Israel has come to Me; furthermore, I have seen the oppression with which the Egyptians are oppressing them. Therefore, come now, and *I will send you to Pharaoh, so that you may bring My people, the sons of Israel, out of Egypt.*" (Exod. 3:9–10, emphasis added)

It was a simple plan. But for Moses, the problem wasn't grasping the concept; it was doing God's will. It was as if God was saying, "Moses, remember that place where you failed miserably? Where the most powerful man in the government wanted you dead and the people you tried to help spit in your face and threatened to squeal on you? I want you to go back there and do exactly what you tried to do before." Have you ever been confronted with returning to the scene of a previous failure? Understandably, Moses didn't want to have anything to do with it.

God, however, didn't ask for Moses' feelings on the subject. He simply told him to go and do as He said. This was not a request, it was a call. God's call is like that today—it's not optional or multiple choice. It's a well-defined, specifically arranged declaration to which there is only one right response.

Moses, though, apparently misconstrued the divine command.

> But Moses said to God, "Who am I, that I should go to Pharaoh, and that I should bring the sons of Israel out of Egypt?" (v. 11)

Moses seemed to think God wanted him to be Israel's deliverer, but God intended him to be only an instrument through which He Himself would deliver the Hebrews. Partly out of fear and partly out of misunderstanding, Moses responded with resistance. But God immediately corrected him:

> "Certainly I will be with you, and this shall be the sign to you that it is I who have sent you: when you have brought the people out of Egypt, you shall worship God at this mountain." (v. 12)

Commentator John Durham observes that "who Moses is is not the question; it is rather, who is *with* Moses?"[1] The Lord not only reassures Moses that He will be with him, but He also gives him a prophetic sign—Moses and the freed people would together worship at "this mountain," which is Mount Sinai, also called Mount Horeb. Through this prophecy, the Lord made it clear to Moses that he was His choice for the task.

Moses Resists God

Moses, though, didn't see himself the way God did. He distrusted himself thoroughly, but his distrust hadn't yet led to trust in God.[2] Let's examine Moses' and God's verbal volleying, in which Moses made four excuses and God responded to each with a direct answer.

Excuse Number One: "Who Shall I Say Sent Me?"

Moses first posed a potential scenario to God.

> Then Moses said to God, "Behold, I am going to the sons of Israel, and I will say to them, 'The God of your fathers has sent me to you.' Now they

---

1. John I. Durham, *Exodus*, vol. 3 of *Word Biblical Commentary* (Waco, Tex.: Word Books, Publishers, 1987), p. 33.

2. R. Alan Cole, *Exodus: An Introduction and Commentary*, The Tyndale Old Testament Commentaries series, gen. ed. D. J. Wiseman (Downers Grove, Ill.: InterVarsity Press, 1973), p. 68.

may say to me, 'What is His name?' What shall I say to them?" (v. 13)

Why would Moses ask this question? He may have been worried about not having all the answers. We often worry about the same thing, and we let it stop us from obeying God's call. But that's only part of it.

Moses and the Hebrews already knew God's name; they would have known "the God of Abraham, the God of Isaac, and the God of Jacob" (v. 6). What they needed to know, in light of their hundreds of years of bondage and suffering, was the nature and character of their God. Was He God of the past only? Had He forgotten about His people? Could He help them now?

Moses is asking, in essence, "What is there in the name of God that will help us in circumstances like these?"[3] Patiently and thoroughly, God told him.

Answer Number One: "I Am Who I Am"

> God said to Moses, "I AM WHO I AM"; and He said, "Thus you shall say to the sons of Israel, 'I AM has sent me to you.'" God, furthermore, said to Moses, "Thus you shall say to the sons of Israel, 'The Lord, the God of your fathers, the God of Abraham, the God of Isaac, and the God of Jacob, has sent me to you.' This is My name forever, and this is My memorial-name to all generations." (vv. 14–15)

In Hebrew, God's name "I AM" is written only with the consonants YHWH, which we commonly pronounce as "Yahweh."[4] I AM comes from the Hebrew verb for "to be"; so the name YHWH is not only a declaration of God's eternal and unchanging self-existence; it also communicates His presence with us. "Yahweh Is," commentator Robert Durham notes,

> However absent he may have seemed to the oppressed Israelites in Egypt, as to the later generations

3. Walter C. Kaiser Jr., "Exodus," in *The Expositor's Bible Commentary*, gen. ed. Frank E. Gaebelein (Grand Rapids, Mich.: Zondervan Publishing House, Academic and Professional Books, 1990), vol. 2, p. 320.

4. The Jews revered God's name so highly that they did not speak it. Instead, they replaced it with *Adonai*, which means "Lord."

for whom the Book of Exodus was compiled, Yahweh Is, and his Is-ness means Presence. . . . This God who is present, this God who Is, this Yahweh, is one and the same as the God of the fathers.[5]

The God who had covenanted with Abraham, Isaac, and Jacob had not forgotten His people or His promises. That same God would be with the Israelites as He was in the past and as He promised He would be with Moses (v. 12). And His wasn't a passive presence but an active, redeeming one that had "seen the affliction of My people," "given heed to their cry," was "aware of their sufferings," and "sent" Moses to them (vv. 7, 14). For these reasons, His name YHWH would "be the medium of continuous worship"[6] for all time.

The Lord then told Moses what to tell the Israelites (vv. 16–22). First, that He was concerned about them and what the Egyptians had done to them. Second, that He would deliver them to a land of their own, "flowing with milk and honey." Third, that Pharaoh would resist, so God would overcome him and his kingdom with miraculous power. And fourth, that Israel would plunder Egypt, because Egypt had mercilessly plundered God's people.

Excuse Number Two: "What If They Will Not Believe Me?"

Surely, after all God had told him, Moses wasn't still afraid. Or was he?

> "What if they will not believe me or listen to what I say? For they may say, 'The Lord has not appeared to you.'" (4:1)

Moses obviously had a clear memory of the Hebrews' knack for not listening to or trusting people. The last time he tried to help, they ran him out of town. If God wanted him to go back, He needed to provide Moses with some solid, verifiable proof that he was coming as God's messenger. Moses was concerned that the people would doubt his credibility and challenge his authority because, personally, they had no reason to respect him.

This sounds practical, but it reveals Moses' increasing resistance. Hadn't God just promised him, "They will pay heed to what you

---

5. Durham, *Exodus*, p. 39.

6. Brevard S. Childs, *The Book of Exodus: A Critical, Theological Commentary*, The Old Testament Library series (Philadelphia, Pa.: Westminster Press, 1974), p. 77.

say" (3:18)? Now Moses was doubting—"Are they *really* going to heed what I say?"

Answer Number Two: "But You'll Have All of My Power"

God reassured Moses by showing him how He would make the Hebrews and Egyptians listen to him. The Lord promised three miraculous signs: turning Moses' staff into a snake and back again, turning his hand leprous and then healthy again, and, finally, turning some Nile water into blood as it was poured on the ground (4:2–9). The third sign would act as a reserve, in case the people refused to accept the other two miracles. In short, the Lord assured Moses that he could count on His power to back up his words. That would surely give Moses all of the credibility, authority, and respect he needed.

Excuse Number Three: "I Don't Have All of the Ability"

Unfortunately, Moses wasn't finished resisting God's will just yet.

> Then Moses said to the Lord, "Please, Lord, I have never been eloquent, neither recently nor in time past, nor since You have spoken to Your servant; for I am slow of speech and slow of tongue." (v. 10)

God's ears must have been ringing! Did Moses have that bad a memory? In Egypt, he had been a powerful public speaker, being a "man of power in words and deeds" (Acts 7:22b). Maybe he felt that, during his forty years in the desert, his talents had withered so much that it was as if he had never had them at all. Whatever the reason, Moses obviously felt inadequate to carry out the task to which God was calling him.

Answer Number Three: "But You Will Have All That Is Needed"

The Lord's response was not only direct but therapeutic:

> "Who has made man's mouth? Or who makes him mute or deaf, or seeing or blind? Is it not I, the Lord? Now then go, and I, even I, will be with your mouth, and teach you what you are to say." (Exod. 4:11–12)

Moses didn't need a refresher course in oratory skills. What he really needed was to trust God's ability and His promise to supplement his weaknesses with divine strength.

Excuse Number Four: *"Someone Else Would Do a Better Job"*

The New International Version captures Moses' thoughts well: "O Lord, please send someone else to do it" (v. 13). The bottom line was that Moses didn't want to go back to Egypt, no matter who God was and what He was offering. He couldn't seem to get past his own inferiority and incapability.

Answer Number Four: *"But You Are My Choice . . . However, I Will Send Another Person along with You"*

This final excuse was the last mouthful of hot air God could stand from Moses. His anger "burned against Moses," but instead of chastising him, He met him where he was by commissioning Aaron to be his spokesman (vv. 14–17). In the presence of Moses' weakness, God provided a helper. In our own times of weakness, God finds ways to help us accept His calling. Instead of punishing us, He provides for us.

Our Response to God

We can resist God's will or we can submit to it. The choice is ours. But once we begin heeding His call, our acceptance needs to be marked by three traits.

First, *certainty that it is God's voice.* We need to make sure we're listening to God and not simply trying to fulfill our own personal desires. The best place to start is the Bible. A wise man once said, "Too many people try to figure out what God is saying without looking at what He has already said."[7] God wants all Christians to live according to biblical standards, and anything we consider to be God's will should be screened through the filter of Scripture.

Second, *confidence in God's power.* Once we verify that a direction is God's call, our next task is to work and trust in His power, not our own. We're never sufficient to handle His tasks, and He never asks us to be. Instead, He provides His own power and sufficiency to our calling so that we can be, as clay pots, human vessels housing divine power (see 2 Cor. 4:7).

Third, *comfort with His plan.* If we learn anything from this episode in Moses' life, let's understand that we should never resist or try to alter God's call. Our circumstances work out far better

---

7. As told to the author by Jackson Shepherd in a conversation in December 1987.

when we are willing to receive what God gives, lack what He withholds, relinquish what He takes, suffer what He inflicts, and become what He requires.

"Who, me, Lord?" Have you ever asked that question? Most of us probably have. When He calls us back after a failure, most of us enter His presence with a reluctant heart and a load of fears strapped over our shoulders. It's time to cut those fears loose and let God use us once again.

 Living Insights

Let's talk about the whole matter of resistance. You might even want to explore this issue with a group of your friends or family. Whether with a group or alone, consider the following questions.[8]

How do you demonstrate resistance to God?

_____

_____

_____

How important is it to you to have all the answers?

_____

_____

_____

How do you handle feelings raised by the fear of not having the respect of others?

_____

_____

_____

8. These questions have been taken from the previous edition of our study guide on Moses, *Moses: God's Man for a Crisis*, coauthored by Bill Watkins, with Living Insights by Bill Butterworth, from the Bible-teaching ministry of Charles R. Swindoll (Fullerton, Calif.: Insight for Living, 1985), p. 38.

What qualifies a person to be effectively used by God?

_____

_____

_____

_____

What are some ways to be certain you are hearing God's voice?

_____

_____

_____

_____

How do you appropriate God's power in your life?

_____

_____

_____

Based on what we've learned about God in this lesson, why should we be comfortable with His plan?

_____

_____

_____

_____

_____

_____

_____

Chapter 8

GOD'S WILL, GOD'S WAY

Exodus 4:18–31

Moses approached Jethro's tent, having just bedded down the livestock for the night. Shadows melted into the dusk, and a soft pink hue settled over the encampment. Midian surely had its moments of beauty. Moses entered the tent, dropping the goatskin flap behind him.

Jethro was lounging by the clay firepot. Moses joined him, bracing his sore, eighty-year-old back as he knelt on the thick pelt next to the fire.

"You're starting to hold your back like an old man," Jethro quipped.

Moses grinned. "I'm as strong as a horse," he replied, "at least as strong smelling!" The two men chuckled at the old Midianite joke.

For Jethro, a companionable silence followed, as he stared contentedly into the fire. But Moses' thoughts were less serene. *How will this dear man react to my request?* he wondered. Moses had rehearsed his words on the way back from the burning bush over and over. But all that practice seemed futile now as he waited for the right moment to speak.

An intrusive wind slapped the door flap in and out. Moses knew the perfect moment would never come; there was no use waiting any longer.

"I have a request," he said softly, the gravity in his voice reflected by his somber expression. Jethro returned his gaze and then looked down.

"What is it, my son?" Jethro fixed his eyes on a spot on the floor and hoped his distant stare would make the words easier to bear.

"I need to know if my people are still alive. Please let me return to Egypt."

Both men stared into the clay pot as the embers glowed, the heat rippling back and forth.

Then Jethro raised his head and looked deep into his son-in-law's eyes. He blinked, and tears rolled down both cheeks. Moses knew what he was asking this man to give up—his daughter and the two grandsons she'd given him.

"Shalom," he said to Moses. "Go, and may my blessing help you on your way."

Then he looked away again, and Moses stood quietly to leave. Jethro needed some time to himself.

A Priority and a Promise

> Trust in the Lord with all your heart
> And do not lean on your own understanding.
> In all your ways acknowledge Him,
> And He will make your paths straight. (Prov. 3:5–6)

Somewhere between the burning bush and Jethro's tent, Moses stopped resisting God and began resting in Him. Instead of leaning on the crutches of his own understanding, he answered God's call to return to Egypt, trusting Him with all his heart—not halfheartedly, but totally without reservation. He leapt out in faith with both feet.

In Exodus 4:18–31, we'll see how God made His servant's "paths straight," removing the stones that would cause Moses to stumble as he followed Him. Sometimes He did this tenderly, sometimes firmly; but as long as Moses acknowledged that God was in charge, God cleared the path before him.

Does this principle imply that our circumstances will always work out the way we want them to when we put God first? Of course not. This truth was never meant to lead us to believe that we can manipulate or bargain with God. It does assure us, though, that no matter what negative situations we face, God will lead us through them if we follow His lead and trust Him totally. Just as He did for Moses.

Moses' Explanation to Jethro

Did you notice the way Moses approached Jethro? Was it the way he would confront Pharaoh—with commands tumbling from his lips? Not at all. His words were humble and respectful.

> "Please, let me go, that I may return to my brethren who are in Egypt, and see if they are still alive." (4:18a)

What a gracious tone of voice for the man who just returned from the very presence of God! No commands. No ultimatums. Not even a word to Jethro about God's divine summons. Instead, Moses showed great wisdom, sensitivity, and faith in his approach. He wisely recognized that Jethro had not seen the burning bush himself—he didn't know all that Moses knew. And Moses understood that he was about to ask his father-in-law to give up his daughter and two grandsons, so he approached the issue gently. Finally, he showed respect to Jethro by phrasing his desire as a request instead of a demand,[1] trusting God for the outcome. How did God respond to Moses' faith? Listen to Jethro's response.

> And Jethro said to Moses, "Go in peace." (v. 18c)

"Go in peace" forms a beautiful expression in Hebrew, which includes the well-known term *shalom*. Through the use of this word, Jethro not only gave Moses permission to leave, but he also gave him his blessing. The family ties, rather than being severed, were supported in grace—Moses couldn't have asked for a smoother road.

However, he still struggled with fear regarding a return to Egypt. You might remember that the last time he was there, several powerful people wanted him dead. Once again, God straightened his path.

---

1. As a legal member of the family, it was customary to gain permission from the father-in-law to move away. Moses honored Jethro by obeying this custom. See note on Exodus 4:18, in *The Nelson Study Bible*, ed. Earl D. Radmacher (Nashville, Tenn.: Thomas Nelson Publishers, 1997), p. 105.

Now the Lord said to Moses in Midian, "Go back to Egypt, for all the men who were seeking your life are dead." (v. 19)[2]

How gracious of God to relieve Moses' worry. Isn't it comforting to know that God wants to encourage us and make following Him a little easier? With the way before him smoothed, Moses was now able to start making preparations to leave.

Moses' Trip to Egypt

So Moses took his wife and his sons and mounted them on a donkey, and returned to the land of Egypt. Moses also took the staff of God in his hand. (v. 20)

Did you notice how the verse describes Moses' staff? It was no longer just the staff of a simple shepherd. In fact, it no longer belonged to the shepherd at all. Rather, it became the possession of God. This was the same staff that the Lord had turned into the snake in 4:2–4 and that He would continue to use as a symbol of His presence in Moses' mission (vv. 5, 17).

God acts similarly in our lives today by taking possession of the things we use for His glory, whether it be our voice in witnessing or singing, our hands in acts of service, or our home when we open it to host small groups or Bible studies. We give those possessions to Him, and He takes them for His purposes. So Moses took the staff of God in his hand and headed for Egypt.

Complete Trust

God's next words were a reminder of something He had told Moses at the burning bush, reiterated here to keep His servant from becoming disillusioned in his task.

The Lord said to Moses, "When you go back to Egypt see that you perform before Pharaoh all the

2. Shadows of Christ are revealed frequently in Moses' life, and these words of the Lord's provide only one example. Commentator R. Alan Cole observes, "God's word to Moses . . . is couched in language that is echoed in Matthew 2:20, with reference to Herod's death. As Moses is also God's chosen instrument, and has had a miraculous deliverance from death, the parallel is the more appropriate." Looking ahead to Exodus 4:20, Cole adds, "Here is an earlier 'holy family' going by donkey to Egypt (cf. Mt. 2:13)." *Exodus: An Introduction and Commentary*, The Tyndale Old Testament Commentaries series (Downers Grove, Ill.: Inter-Varsity Press, 1974), pp. 76–77.

wonders which I have put in your power; but I will harden his heart so that he will not let the people go." (v. 21; see also 3:19–20)

Why would the Lord empower Moses to perform a multitude of miracles only to harden Pharaoh's heart to them? Was God working against Himself? Was this fair to Pharaoh? The apostle Paul grappled with these questions and came up with this answer:

There is no injustice with God, is there? May it never be! . . . For the Scripture says to Pharaoh, "For this very purpose I raised you up, to demonstrate My power in you, and that My name might be proclaimed throughout the whole earth." (Rom. 9:14, 17; see also Exod. 9:16)

Pharaoh, in his arrogance, proclaimed himself divine, but soon he and all the people who worshiped him would know beyond doubt who the true God was. And Pharaoh's own stubbornness would be a tool in accomplishing God's purpose. As God continued telling Moses:

"Then you shall say to Pharaoh, 'Thus says the Lord, "Israel is My son, My firstborn. So I said to you, 'Let My son go that he may serve Me'; but you have refused to let him go. Behold, I will kill your son, your firstborn."'" (Exod. 4:22–23)

Essentially, God was telling Moses to say to the world's most powerful man, "God told you to let the Hebrews, His preeminent and beloved people, go, and you refused. Now He will kill your firstborn." Here God forewarned Pharaoh of His final, most catastrophic plague—a prophecy the Egyptian ruler chose to see before he would believe.

But look at Moses' response—there isn't one. We might have expected Moses to ask questions or argue with God again. But he didn't. He simply listened to God and obeyed with a quiet confidence. In other words, he trusted God with all his heart, accepting what may very well have been inscrutable to him (see Rom. 11:33).

Complete Obedience

Once God brings us to the point of trusting Him totally and without reservation, He then deals with areas in our lives we've neglected. He certainly did with Moses, as the servant-leader began his journey back to Egypt.

> Now it came about at the lodging place on the way that the Lord met him and sought to put him to death. Then Zipporah took a flint and cut off her son's foreskin and threw it at Moses' feet, and she said, "You are indeed a bridegroom of blood to me." So He let him alone. At that time she said, "You are a bridegroom of blood"—because of the circumcision. (Exod. 4:24–26)

Apparently, Moses had disobeyed one of God's most important commands by failing to circumcise one of his sons. God must have incapacitated him, because it was Zipporah who circumcised the boy. Her act of throwing the foreskin down perhaps indicated that she was repulsed by this rite. But their obedience, forced as it was, stayed God's wrath and saved Moses' life.[3]

Possibly, Moses was the only family member able to continue the trip to Egypt. The rest of the family might have returned to Midian so that the newly circumcised boy could recover (compare 18:1–5).

Moses' Encounter with Aaron

With Moses alone, the Lord directed Aaron, who was already on his way (4:14), to meet him in the desert. Aaron found him at Mount Sinai, "the mountain of God," and greeted him warmly "and kissed him" (4:27). Moses then told Aaron "all the words of the Lord with which He had sent him, and all the signs that He had commanded him to do" (v. 28). This marks the first recorded incident where Moses told someone about his commissioning at the burning bush. Since Aaron had also been "commissioned" by God to partner with Moses in delivering the Hebrews (vv. 15–16), it was important that he learn all that God had told his younger brother.

Moses and Aaron's Initial Experience with the Hebrews

Upon arriving in Egypt, Moses and Aaron "assembled all the

---

3. Ronald F. Youngblood points out that "before Moses could return to Egypt to rescue the covenant people as their acknowledged leader, he himself must obey the covenant in every detail." *Exodus*, Everyman's Bible Commentary series (Chicago, Ill.: Moody Press, 1983), p. 38.

elders of the sons of Israel" (v. 29). Then "Aaron spoke all the words which the Lord had spoken to Moses. He [Moses] then performed the signs in the sight of the people" (v. 30). The event that followed occurred exactly as the Lord had predicted.

> So the people believed; and when they heard that the Lord was concerned about the sons of Israel and that He had seen their affliction, then they bowed low and worshiped. (v. 31)

The same people who had once refused to follow Moses' lead now believed that he was God's instrument of deliverance. But more importantly, the people whose affliction had crushed their hope now saw the light of God's care and deliverance . . . and they worshiped the God who was present with them.

 Living Insights

Moses—at first rash and impetuous in trying to free his people; then so shaken by his failure that he tried to wriggle away from God's explicit charge to deliver the Hebrews. Finally, though, he took his eyes off himself, trusted God, and obeyed Him. There's an old hymn that captures the essence of his experience called "Trust and Obey." Take some time to read the first stanza and chorus, allowing the words to feed your soul as you reflect on your long trek of obedience.

> When we walk with the Lord
> In the light of His Word,
> What a glory He sheds on our way!
> While we do His good will
> He abides with us still,
> And with all who will trust and obey.

> [Chorus] Trust and obey—
> For there's no other way
> To be happy in Jesus
> But to trust and obey.[4]

---

4. John H. Sammis, "Trust and Obey," in *Great Hymns of the Faith*, comp. and ed. John W. Peterson (Grand Rapids, Mich.: Zondervan Publishing House, Singspiration, 1968), no. 261.

Have you had a time in your life when you struggled against God's will? What were some of the reasons for your struggle?

_____

_____

_____

_____

_____

Did you get to a place where you finally trusted God and obeyed Him? Did you "have all the answers" before this happened? Or was there quite a bit of faith involved?

_____

_____

_____

_____

Did God prove Himself faithful when you trusted Him and obeyed His will? Did you sense His faithful, righteous, and present care?

_____

_____

_____

_____

Have you thanked and worshiped Him, as the Hebrews did (Exod. 4:31), for being your "refuge and strength, A very present help in trouble" (Ps. 46:1)? If not, do so now. And if you already have, praise Him for the memory of His faithfulness, for having made "your paths straight" (Prov. 3:6b).

Chapter 9
GOING FROM BAD TO WORSE
Exodus 5–6

Have you ever had a day that started out on the wrong foot, then went from bad to worse? On days like that, most of us wish we'd never gotten out of bed. That's how Moses felt the day he confronted Pharaoh the first time.

Moses had been riding the crest of a wave of confidence, with he and Aaron having received the full support and faith of the Hebrew elders. They had performed miracles and spoken powerfully. They were rested and ready. But then they ran smack into a stubborn, arrogant, and cruel Pharaoh, who started a chain of reactions that just went from bad to worse. Without a doubt, this was a day they wished they'd pulled the covers over their heads and stayed put.

Pharaoh's Response to Moses

Pharaoh's response initiated a set of three cycles, each following a set pattern: an announcement, a reaction, resulting anger, and unjust blame. Moses and Aaron might have started out confident, but by the time Pharaoh got done with them, even they were doubting God.

Cycle One

Following their uplifting spiritual conference with the Hebrew elders (Exod. 4:29–31), Moses and Aaron boldly stood before Pharaoh and proclaimed God's word.

> "Thus says the Lord, the God of Israel, 'Let My people go that they may celebrate a feast to Me in the wilderness.'" (5:1)

But Pharaoh refused to sit idly by as these two goatherds threw down ultimatums. His reaction dripped with sarcasm.

> "Who is the Lord that I should obey His voice to let Israel go? I do not know the Lord, and besides, I will not let Israel go." (v. 2b)

In essence, Pharoah was saying, "I am the 'Lord' of Egypt, and the people will serve me." So Moses and Aaron shrewdly softened their demand by putting it in the form of a request (v. 3; see 3:18), perhaps hoping God would then soften Pharaoh's heart. But with greater anger than before, Pharaoh again refused to grant their petition. Only this time, he revealed his real motive for not permitting the Hebrews to leave—he was afraid to lose his large labor force (5:4–5). He looked out at the slaves, blamed Moses and Aaron for taking them away from their work, and issued his infamous command.

> So the same day Pharaoh commanded the taskmasters over the people and their foremen, saying, "You are no longer to give the people straw to make brick as previously; let them go and gather straw for themselves. But the quota of bricks which they were making previously, you shall impose on them; you are not to reduce any of it. Because they are lazy, therefore they cry out, 'Let us go and sacrifice to our God.' Let the labor be heavier on the men, and let them work at it that they will pay no attention to false words." (vv. 6–9)

Moses and Aaron had hit a snag in the plan. Their announcement received an unbelieving response from Pharaoh; then he lashed out at the Hebrew slaves with tyrannical anger, all the while blaming Moses and Aaron's "false words." With the chain of events set in motion, things were about to go from bad to worse.

Cycle Two

The Egyptian taskmasters and the Hebrew foremen under them announced this ruthless new command to the people:

> "Thus says Pharaoh, 'I am not going to give you any straw. You go and get straw for yourselves wherever you can find it, but none of your labor will be reduced.'" (vv. 10–11)

Despite their best efforts to obey (v. 12), the Hebrews were unable to do the impossible. So Pharaoh's taskmasters beat their foremen and blamed them for their people's failure.

> "Why have you not completed your required amount either yesterday or today in making brick as previously?" (v. 14b)

69

The Hebrews, however, didn't know why they were being deprived of straw. That is, until they decided to take the matter up with Pharaoh.

Cycle Three

> Then the foremen of the sons of Israel came and cried out to Pharaoh, saying, "Why do you deal this way with your servants? There is no straw given to your servants, yet they keep saying to us, 'Make bricks!' And behold, your servants are being beaten; but it is the fault of your own people." (vv. 15–16)

In their ignorance, the Israelites actually complained to Pharaoh! They thought the lack of straw was due to laziness on the part of the Egyptian workers who had been providing it, and they announced that fact to Egypt's ruler. But they were about to be blindsided with the truth.

> [Pharaoh] said, "You are lazy, very lazy; therefore you say, 'Let us go and sacrifice to the Lord.' So go now and work; for you will be given no straw, yet you must deliver the quota of bricks." (vv. 17–18)

Can you see the wheels turning inside the foremen's heads as they started to read between the lines? *Who would have talked to Pharaoh about leaving Egypt to worship Yahweh? Only two people fit this description: Moses and Aaron.*

Moses and Aaron sat outside the palace gates, waiting for the Hebrew elders. The sweltering sun bleached every sandstone surface, and the two men shaded their eyes. They squatted on the side of the road trying to pass the time, Aaron fingering a pebble in the dirt and Moses jabbing pockmarks in the road with his staff.

"They looked pretty beat up," Aaron said, referring to the elders' appearance when they entered the palace. The Egyptian overseers had whipped them for missing their quota of bricks.

"Yes," Moses said. "Did you get a close look at Jethriel's eye?" He thrust the end of the staff into the hole, then twisted the rod so that the loosened dirt squirted out the sides. "I can't even imagine the weapon that would make that kind of welt."

"I don't know either, but they must have hit him pretty hard to make the white of his eye turn red like that."

Moses nodded in agreement. He stopped jabbing the dirt, lost in his thoughts. This was the time the Lord had appointed; he was sure of it. He had expected Pharaoh to reject his request—God had foretold that much. But would Pharaoh take the offensive and brutalize the Hebrews because of him? Surely not! God would have prepared him if that were part of the plan.

"You don't think," Aaron asked, "the beatings had anything to do with us, do you?"

Moses paused. "I think they did."

Just then, the palace gates opened and the foremen came out. Moses and Aaron stood up and stepped into the road to meet them. The foremen looked angry.

The foremen blamed Moses and Aaron for their new dilemma.

> They said to them, "May the Lord look upon you and judge you, for you have made us odious in Pharaoh's sight and in the sight of his servants, to put a sword in their hand to kill us." (v. 21)

"Worse" never felt so bad. In less than a day, their hopes for an immediate deliverance were dashed. Moses didn't understand what had happened any more than the others. There was only one thing left for him to do.

Moses' Response to God

He complained to God. After all, he was finally doing God's will, God's way—and yet everything still went wrong! This was no better than the first time, when he ended up fleeing to Midian. Pharaoh not only slammed the door on his request but also tightened the screws of oppression on his people—and they just loved him for that. Moses' complaint came in the form of two familiar questions every believer asks at some point.

"Why?"

> Then Moses returned to the Lord and said, "O Lord, why have You brought harm to this people? Why did You ever send me? Ever since I came to Pharaoh to speak in Your name, he has done harm to this people, and You have not delivered Your people at all." (vv. 22–23)

The third word out of Moses' mouth was *why?* God had warned him that Pharaoh would resist (3:19–20; 4:21). Moses, however, didn't understand why the Lord was allowing Pharaoh to take the offensive. Perhaps he wondered why God, who intended to free the Hebrews, would allow their suffering to increase. But God responded with a promise of action.

> Then the Lord said to Moses, "Now you shall see what I will do to Pharaoh; for under compulsion he will let them go, and under compulsion he will drive them out of his land." (6:1)

The Lord also reiterated the trustworthiness of His identity, covenant, and care, and He reassured Moses that He would indeed keep His promise to deliver His people and bring them to the land He had promised to their fathers (vv. 2–8).

In good faith, then, Moses returned to the Hebrews and told them the new message of hope from the Lord. "But they did not listen to Moses on account of their despondency and cruel bondage" (v. 9). This failure sent Moses right back into despair, and right back to the Lord.

"How?"

But Moses spoke before the Lord, saying, "Behold, the sons of Israel have not listened to me; how then will Pharaoh listen to me, for I am unskilled in speech?" (v. 12)

Do you see what Moses was doing? He was taking the responsibility to free the Hebrews on himself, and he was blaming himself for failing. In particular, he criticized his lack of eloquence as the cause for his inability to rally the Hebrews. He also wondered aloud that if he couldn't persuade his own people to listen to him, then how would Pharaoh heed his words (compare vv. 28–30)? Moses was definitely wallowing in a pit of despair.[1]

God's Response to Moses

God did not leave Moses in an emotional lurch with either of his questions. He consoled and counseled him by reminding him about some truths regarding His nature and His will.

"I Am"

Five times in chapter 6 God said to Moses, "I am the Lord [YHWH]" (vv. 2, 6, 7, 8, 29). By repeating His name, God emphasized Moses' need to stay focused on Him and to let Him take responsibility for freeing the Hebrews. Because, as His name attested, He was a covenant-keeping God who would indeed redeem His people. These actions stemmed from His very nature. "I am the Redeemer, so I will redeem you," God said, implying, "so keep your eyes on Me."

---

1. Are you a bit puzzled about why Moses and Aaron's family tree is suddenly dropped into the middle of this story? Commentator John D. Hannah explains that "the genealogy was placed here to identify Moses and Aaron more precisely because of the prominent position they were assuming as representatives of the people before the Egyptian state . . . [and] to focus on . . . their authority to lead the people from Pharaoh's grasp." "Exodus," in *The Bible Knowledge Commentary*, Old Testament edition, ed. John F. Walvoord and Roy B. Zuck (Wheaton, Ill.: Scripture Press Publications, Victor Books, 1985), pp. 117, 118. John I. Durham adds, "This genealogy may be seen as an attempt to set both Aaron and Moses firmly within the special descendancy of Jacob/Israel's third son, Levi, the ancestor of the line of those who handle holy things and mediate Yahweh's words of expectation and judgment. While the original purpose of the passage may have been legitimation, its purpose in its present setting is the celebration of the descendancy of the promise." *Exodus*, Word Biblical Commentary series (Waco, Tex.: Word Books, Publisher, 1987), vol. 3, p. 84.

What was true then is also true now. When things go from bad to worse for us, the only way we can endure is by riveting our attention on the Lord. We need to remember His sovereignty, goodness, power, justice, compassion, love, and nearness—especially when we find ourselves sinking in a bad situation. Because of who God is, we can be confident that He is in control of our circumstances.

"I Will"

Seven times God answered Moses by describing how He would intervene.

> "Say, therefore, to the sons of Israel, 'I am the Lord, and I *will* bring you out from under the burdens of the Egyptians, and I *will* deliver you from their bondage. I *will* also redeem you with an outstretched arm and with great judgments. Then I *will* take you for My people, and I *will* be your God; and you shall know that I am the Lord your God, who brought you out from under the burdens of the Egyptians. I *will* bring you to the land which I swore to give to Abraham, Isaac, and Jacob, and I *will* give it to you for a possession; I am the Lord.'" (vv. 6–8, emphasis added)

Based on these seven "I will" statements, commentator Ronald Youngblood concludes,

> The Exodus therefore became the supreme example of God's activity as Redeemer in the Old Testament. God's irresistible plan and irreversible intention was to bring His people out (of slavery in Egypt) in order to bring them in (to freedom in Canaan). And so we are reminded that redemption is not only release from slavery and suffering but also deliverance to freedom and joy. In addition, God's "mighty acts of judgment" (v. 6; see also Exod. 7:4) involved not only redemption for Israel but also judgment against Egypt.[2]

We can summarize God's message to Moses in verses 2–8 in these words: "Because I am who I am, I will always do what is best

2. Ronald F. Youngblood, *Exodus*, Everyman's Bible Commentary series (Chicago, Ill.: Moody Press, 1983), p. 43.

for you." That's the Lord's message to us as well. If we believe that during those days which go from bad to worse, we will see a marked change in our ability to handle them. With this truth in mind, God sent Moses back to Pharaoh to continue his appointed mission (v. 13), and He asks the same of us.

Our Response to Difficult Circumstances

When we're doing God's will, He never wants us to retreat—not even when our circumstances go from bad to worse. Instead, His desire is for us to stand fast, trusting in who He is and what He has promised to do. He'll provide the victory if we'll act in faith, recalling the truths we've learned from His Word.

The principles from this lesson teach us that tough times can be met with faith and overcome with God's promised presence, and that dependence and patience have their reward. We can sum up what we've learned in the following principles, which build on one another to help us grow when circumstances go from bad to worse.

- *Circumstances that turn against us force dependence.*

- *Circumstances that force dependence teach us patience.*

- *Circumstances that teach us patience make us wise.*

Because God is who He is, He will do what is best for us. Even when things go badly, He provides a way for them to work for our benefit.

 Living Insights

All of us experience at least one period in our Christian walks when circumstances seem to go from bad to worse. Though no two trials are alike, the end of each one can have a singular benefit for the child of God—spiritual endurance.

James 1:2–8 perfectly describes the character-building benefits of struggles. Read this passage several times, and then sit quietly and mull over the truths it contains. Imagine all the different ways you can apply those principles to your life. Consider your relationships and responsibilities in all the different arenas in which you operate, such as work, church, and home. Then write down what the Spirit brings to mind.

Consider it all joy, my brethren, when you encounter various trials, knowing that the testing of your faith produces endurance. And let endurance have its perfect result, so that you may be perfect and complete, lacking in nothing.

But if any of you lacks wisdom, let him ask of God, who gives to all generously and without reproach, and it will be given to him. But he must ask in faith without any doubting, for the one who doubts is like the surf of the sea, driven and tossed by the wind. For that man ought not to expect that he will receive anything from the Lord, being a double-minded man, unstable in all his ways.

_____

_____

_____

_____

_____

_____

_____

_____

_____

_____

_____

_____

_____

_____

_____

Chapter 10

PLAGUES THAT PREACH

Exodus 7–10

*D*o this thing!" Pharaoh ordered.

"We've tried, Majesty, but we can't duplicate the gnats."

He glared at his magicians like an overbearing animal trainer, and they cowered like whipped dogs. Despite the heavy drapes over every palace window and entrance, the gnats flooded in unabated, stinging and swarming and driving everyone to the brink of insanity. Even Pharaoh's eyes were beginning to have the look of a wild, raging animal.

"We can't do it, sire," they repeated. "It must be the finger of God."

"Get out!" he screamed. "I'll beat you to death if you don't get out of my sight right now, you useless fools!"

The magicians ran through the nearest doorway, and Pharaoh spun around and wildly swiped the air near his ears and face. He shuddered as thousands of pin needles crawled over his flesh.

The next morning, Pharaoh and his priests sought relief in the cool waters of the Nile. As he approached the bank, however, he saw Moses standing directly in his path, with staff in hand.

Pharaoh stopped for no man and certainly wouldn't for this Hebrew. He and his entourage strode ahead, trying to brush Moses aside with a stone-faced stare. But Moses stood his ground.

"This is what the Lord says," Moses proclaimed. "'Let My people go so they may serve Me. If you don't, I will swarm you with worse insects—you, your servants, your people, and your houses. Yes, the Egyptians' houses will be alive with insects, and the ground will crawl with them.'"

Pharaoh stopped in his tracks. But Moses continued.

"'However,' the Lord said, 'I will make a distinction on that day between Goshen, where My people live, and Egypt. No insects will swarm there so that you may know that I, the Lord, am present in this land. I will distinguish My people from your people, and you'll see this sign tomorrow.'"

No more swarms, Pharaoh pleaded silently in his heart, *no more swarms!* But then he remembered the other reason he had come to the river—to plead with Hapi. Everyone knew that Egypt belonged to Hapi, and no foreign gods had ever held sway in Hapi's land. This little Hebrew deity would soon learn his lesson. Pharaoh's neck stiffened and his shoulders tensed.

"Bring on your insects, nomad," he said, "and then witness what Hapi will do to your Lord's precious land of Goshen!"

Pharaoh threw his cape over his shoulder, marched past Moses, and continued to the Nile.

Prelude to the Plagues

Is this bold Moses the same Moses we saw in our last chapter? When we left him, he was struggling to understand why God hadn't snapped His fingers and delivered the Hebrews after his and Aaron's first confrontation with Pharaoh. He had doubted his calling and abilities, and he had even dared to chide the Lord (5:22–23; 6:12, 30). What changed him? Let's go back and see.

The Lord said to Moses, "'See, I make you as God to Pharaoh, and your brother Aaron shall be your prophet'" (7:1). God patiently reassured Moses that He was with him. Then He reminded His servant that Pharaoh's hard heart would be hardened some more so that He could multiply His signs and wonders in Egypt, bringing out His people by "great judgments" (vv. 2–4). There would be no more mistaking who was Lord then (v. 5).

To cement the sureness of His promise, God worked a miracle through Moses and Aaron in Pharaoh's presence. Aaron threw down his staff, which not only became a snake but devoured the staff-snakes of the magicians who "duplicated" his "trick." This was a powerful foreshadowing of the great judgments that would soon devour the pride of Egypt (vv. 8–12). And just as the Lord had said, Pharaoh's heart grew ominously hard.

Ten plagues would follow, each worse than the one before. God predicted them at the burning bush—they were no afterthoughts (see 3:19–22; 4:21–23). Pharaoh's own stubborn claim to divinity and sovereignty required the plagues—God's people would serve the true and holy Lord, not the false and cruel lord of Egypt. And Moses' questions were answered by the plagues—he and the Hebrews would know the power and trustworthiness of their Redeemer.

The First Nine Plagues

Since the tenth plague inaugurates God's Passover, we will devote the next chapter to it alone. Let's turn, then, to the first nine, surveying the increasingly troubled terrain the Lord created and communicated through Moses' faltering lips.

We can make two general observations about these plagues. First, each one affected all the Egyptians—God's judgment was thorough. Second, none of them softened Pharaoh's heart. Even though he finally allowed the Hebrews to leave after the tenth plague, he later pursued them to bring them back into slavery.

These first nine plagues, interestingly, can be arranged in groups of three: the first three (blood, frogs, gnats) harassed the people; plagues four through six (insects, livestock disease, boils) caused them pain; and the last three (hail, locusts, darkness) terrified them.

Commentator Ronald Youngblood crystallizes God's purposes in sending these terrible plagues on Egypt.

> The Lord sent the plagues to judge Egypt and her gods (Exod. 7:4; 10:2; 12:12; 18:11) . . . many of the individual plagues seem to have been directed against a specific Egyptian deity. . . . The plagues were also used by God to compel the pharaoh to free the Israelites (7:4; 18:10). Third, they were sent to prove once and for all that God Himself is the only sovereign Lord of nature and history (7:5; 9:14–15; 10:2; 18:11). Fourth, the plagues struck the land of Goshen selectively, making a distinction between Egypt and Israel and demonstrating that the Israelites were God's chosen people, who came under His protective care (8:22–23; 11:7; 12:27). Finally, the plagues displayed the Lord's almighty power and proclaimed His holy name (9:16).[1]

With these purposes in mind, let's now examine each plague.

Plague 1: Blood

"'Pharaoh's heart is stubborn'" (7:14). With these words of the Lord's, the onslaught of the plagues began. God told Moses to station himself at the bank of the Nile and confront Pharaoh with the command to let the Hebrews go to worship their Lord . . . or else (vv. 15–19). Or else what? Moses showed Pharaoh.

> He lifted up the staff and struck the water that was in the Nile, in the sight of Pharaoh and in the sight of his servants, and all the water that was in the Nile was turned to blood. The fish that were in the Nile died, and the Nile became foul, so that the Egyptians could not drink water from the Nile. And the blood was through all the land of Egypt. (vv. 7:20–21)

What a place to begin! The Nile was the centerpiece of Egyptian society. Citizens and slaves alike relied on it for three crucial things: water, food, and bathing. In a mere instant, all three were taken away.

---

1. Ronald F. Youngblood, *Exodus*, Everyman's Bible Commentary series (Chicago, Ill.: Moody Press, 1983), p. 50.

But the attack on the Nile struck even deeper at Egypt's spiritual roots. The Nile god, Hapi, was their supreme deity, and the Egyptians, including Pharaoh, often came to the river to worship him.[2] By turning this life source into a bloody stream of death, the Lord stated unequivocally that He was superior to Egypt's greatest deity.

Pharaoh's magicians, however, replicated this sign through "their secret arts" (v. 22a), cheaply copying the genuine miracle but not reversing it. But their trick was enough to harden Pharaoh's heart, so he disregarded the Lord and let his thirsty people dig around the Nile for water for seven long days (vv. 22b–25).

Plague 2: Frogs

With Pharaoh unmoved by a blood-red Nile and the stench of dead fish, there was only one thing to do: send in the frogs. And this is what God did. Once again, He told Moses to warn Pharaoh to let the Hebrews go so they could worship Him, and if he refused,

> ""Behold, I will smite your whole territory with frogs. The Nile will swarm with frogs, which will come up and go into your house and into your bedroom and on your bed, and into the houses of your servants and on your people, and into your ovens and into your kneading bowls."" (8:2–3)

Why did God choose frogs? John D. Hannah suggests that it was because "the Egyptians regarded frogs as having divine power.

> In the Egyptian pantheon the goddess Heqet had the form of a woman with a frog's head. . . .
> . . . The sacred animals would multiply and infiltrate people's bedrooms. This is ironic since the frog-goddess Heqet was believed to help women in childbirth.[3]

As a further irony, Pharaoh's magicians replicated this miracle, bringing on more frogs—just what Pharaoh needed (v. 7)! Actually, this plague got to him; he told Moses and Aaron to "entreat the

---

2. C. F. Keil and F. Delitzsch, *The Pentateuch*, vol. 1 of *Biblical Commentary on the Old Testament* (Grand Rapids, Mich.: William B. Eerdmans Publishing Co., n.d.), p. 478.

3. John D. Hannah, "Exodus," in *The Bible Knowledge Commentary*, Old Testament edition, ed. John F. Walvoord and Roy B. Zuck (Wheaton, Ill.: Scripture Press Publications, Victor Books, 1985), pp. 121–22.

Lord that He remove the frogs," and he even promised to let the people go and sacrifice to the Lord (v. 8). Moses graciously allowed Pharaoh to set the time—"Tomorrow!"—for the frogs to cease, so that he would "know that there is no one like the Lord our God" (vv. 9–10). And God stopped the frogs all right . . . dead in their tracks. "The land became foul" with the heaps of frogs rotting in the sun. But the relief only hardened Pharaoh further, and he reneged on his promise (vv. 12–15).

Plague 3: Gnats

Since Pharaoh had not heeded the other warnings, this third plague came unannounced.[4]

> Aaron stretched out his hand with his staff, and struck the dust of the earth, and there were gnats on man and beast. All the dust of the earth became gnats through all the land of Egypt. (8:17)

The Hebrew word translated *gnats* could indicate either a species of tiny, stinging insects that would penetrate people's nostrils and eyes,[5] or mosquitoes. In either case, the effect would have been maddening.

Significantly, Pharaoh's magicians from this point on could not copy any more of God's miracles (v. 18). Instead, they confessed to Pharaoh, "This is the finger of God" (v. 19). These are also their last recorded words. Unlike their hard-hearted Pharaoh, they recognized that the God of Moses and Aaron was truly at work; but they obediently stayed by their master's side, silently knowing who would win this battle of wills.

Plague 4: Flies

As we saw in the narrative at the beginning of this chapter, Pharaoh may have been needled by the gnats but not enough to release his stranglehold on the Hebrews. Not even with the threat of swarming insects looming over him. Just as Moses had warned, this hideous mixture of flying insects came the next day and layed waste to the land (v. 24). But not all of the land. For God, remember,

---

4. The last plague in each of the three groups of plagues always comes unannounced (8:16; 9:8–10; 10:21–22).

5. Keil and Delitzsch, *The Pentateuch*, p. 483.

had told Moses to inform Pharaoh that

> """on that day I will set apart the land of Goshen, where My people are living, so that no swarms of insects will be there, in order that you may know that I, the Lord, am in the midst of the land.""" (v. 22)

Commentator Walter Kaiser notes that "gods were thought by ancient Near Easterners to possess no power except on their own home ground. But not so here!"[6] God not only protected His people, but He also afflicted the people "belonging" to other gods—proving His superiority, sovereignty, and omnipotence. From this point on, God will protect the Hebrews from the plagues.

Pharaoh reacted immediately—but not obediently—to the swarms: "Go, sacrifice to your God *within* the land" (v. 25, emphasis added). But Moses held firm to following God's instructions (vv. 26–27). Pharaoh acquiesced, stipulating that they not go very far (v. 28). So Moses agreed to pray for the swarms to leave, but he warned Pharaoh not to "deal deceitfully again in not letting the people go" (v. 29). After God answered the request, though, Pharaoh reneged once more (vv. 31–32).

Plague 5: Livestock Epidemic

How much more of Egypt would Pharaoh's obstinance destroy? He would soon see. The Lord next told Moses,

> "Go to Pharaoh and speak to him, 'Thus says the Lord, the God of the Hebrews, "Let My people go, that they may serve Me. For if you refuse to let them go and continue to hold them, behold, the hand of the Lord will come with a very severe pestilence on your livestock which are in the field, on the horses, on the donkeys, on the camels, on the herds, and on the flocks.""" (9:1–3)

God had already destroyed their supply of fish when He turned the Nile to blood. Now He was threatening to destroy the animals that provided not only their meat but also their clothing and livelihoods. After this plague, there couldn't have been much food left

---

6. Walter C. Kaiser Jr., "Exodus," in *The Expositor's Bible Commentary*, gen. ed. Frank E. Gaebelein (Grand Rapids, Mich.: Zondervan Publishing House, Academic and Professional Books, 1990), vol. 2, p. 355.

in Egypt. But even after seeing the livestock of the Lord's people alive and well in Goshen, Pharaoh still refused to bow to God's command (vv. 5–7).

Plague 6: Boils

So the Lord sent Moses and Aaron with yet another plague, which, like the third one, came without any verbal warning (vv. 8–9).

> They took soot from a kiln, and stood before Pharaoh; and Moses threw it toward the sky, and it became boils breaking out with sores on man and beast. (v. 10)

The soot from the brick-kiln of the Hebrews' slavery was turned by God into an affliction for the enslavers. Even the Egyptian magicians couldn't escape the sores (v. 11). And for the first time, we are told that it was the Lord who hardened Pharaoh's heart (v. 12).

Plague 7: Hail

With frightening directness, God through Moses told Pharaoh, "This time I will send the full force of my plagues against you and against your officials and your people, so you may know that there is no one like me in all the earth" (v. 14 NIV). These words signaled the beginning of the third, and most severe, cycle of the first nine plagues, which started with the terrifying destruction of a massive hailstorm (v. 18).

> Moses stretched out his staff toward the sky, and the Lord sent thunder and hail, and fire ran down to the earth. And the Lord rained hail on the land of Egypt. So there was hail, and fire flashing continually in the midst of the hail, very severe, such as had not been in all the land of Egypt since it became a nation. The hail struck all that was in the field through all the land of Egypt, both man and beast; the hail also struck every plant of the field and shattered every tree of the field. (vv. 23–25)

Only the land of Goshen and those Egyptians who heeded God's counsel to seek shelter escaped the vicious storm (vv. 19–20, 26). Pharaoh, for the first time, appeared to be broken and repentant, unconditionally promising to release the Hebrews (vv. 27–28). Moses knew better than to trust him but interceded anyway

(vv. 29–33). Once the hailstorm ceased, however, Pharaoh "sinned again and hardened his heart" (vv. 34–35).

Plague 8: Locusts

God next told Moses to go again to Pharaoh—whose heart God Himself hardened this time in order to "'make a mockery of the Egyptians'" and their pride, unjust power, and false gods. But He also added, "'that you'"—God's people—"'may know that I am the Lord'" (10:1–2). What message would Moses bring? One of severe judgment, a plague dreaded the world over: locusts.

> The locusts came up over all the land of Egypt and settled in all the territory of Egypt; they were very numerous. There had never been so many locusts, nor would there be so many again. For they covered the surface of the whole land, so that the land was darkened; and they ate every plant of the land and all the fruit of the trees that the hail had left. Thus nothing green was left on tree or plant of the field through all the land of Egypt. (vv. 14–15)

Pharaoh's servants had asked him, "Do you not realize that Egypt is destroyed?" (v. 7). In the devastating aftermath of the locusts, he apparently did. He "hurriedly called for Moses and Aaron" and confessed his sin (vv. 16–17). But when Moses interceded in prayer and the locusts were removed, "the Lord hardened Pharaoh's heart, and he did not let the sons of Israel go" (vv. 19–20).

Plague 9: Darkness

The ninth plague, like the third and sixth, came without warning. God told Moses,

> "Stretch out your hand toward the sky, that there may be darkness over the land of Egypt, even a darkness which may be felt." (v. 21)

Lasting three days, this darkness was so great that the Egyptians couldn't see one another or do anything (vv. 22–23a). But the Israelites had light (v. 23b). In response, Pharaoh told Moses, "Go, serve the Lord; only let your flocks and your herds be detained. Even your little ones may go with you" (v. 24).

But when Moses stipulated that he must release the livestock as well, "the Lord hardened Pharaoh's heart" so that he once again refused to let them go (vv. 25–27). Pharaoh then delivered a belligerent tirade against Moses: "Get away from me! Beware, do not see my face again, for in the day you see my face you shall die!" (v. 28).

But Moses stood before him unafraid. With authority in his voice, he said, "You are right; I shall never see your face again!" (v. 29). Moses knew that death would come, but not to a Hebrew.

 ## Living Insights

This account of God's judgment hasn't been recorded and preserved simply for the sake of history or for morbid curiosity. It's been written to give us a deeper knowledge of God. Of the many lessons we could draw from this text, let's focus on the following two.

First, *when God judges, He does a thorough job.* Would you say God performed a comprehensive judgment on Egypt? Understatement of the year! But through all the judging, we also saw God's merciful purposes and patience in the plagues. What were God's purposes? (For help, review Exod. 7:5, 17a; 8:10, 22; 9:14b, 16, 29b; 10:1–2.)

_____

_____

_____

_____

_____

Unfortunately, most of the Egyptians refused to acknowledge, submit to, or obey the Lord. And the same is true of many people today. They believe God exists but don't want anyone holding them accountable for their behavior. What light do the plagues shed on the eternal fate of those who stubbornly refuse to turn to God?

_____

_____

_____

_____

_____

On the flip side, as we saw in Exodus, God waits patiently for even the most stubborn people to bow down to Him. If you were a Moses for today, what message would God have you proclaim to your world (see John 3:16–17 for starters)?

_____

_____

_____

Second, *when God blesses, He holds nothing back.* While God inflicted Egypt with the severe disasters of His judgment, He shielded the Hebrews for their day of deliverance. What does that tell you about God's care?

_____

_____

_____

About His promise to keep His word?

_____

_____

_____

About His justice?

_____

_____

_____

We may think of *judgment* as an ugly word, especially in our overtolerant society. But God's judgments reflect His flawless justice, His perfect standards of right and wrong. The plagues in Exodus 7–10 clearly and graphically display His condemnation of wrong and His deliverance of the oppressed who look to Him for help.

We have one more plague to go—the most devastating to those who choose to be God's enemies. But for those who trust in His deliverance, this plague is a symbol of His grace.

The Plagues of God and the Gods of Egypt: Exodus 7–12

	Plagues	Warnings	Extent	Pharaoh's Responses	Egyptian Deities Most Likely Targeted by the Plagues
1.	Water turned to blood (7:14–25)	Given to Pharaoh (7:15–18, 20a)	"All the land of Egypt" (7:21b)	Hardened his heart, refused to listen, displayed indifference (7:22b–23)	Hapi—god of the Nile Isis—goddess of the Nile Khnum—guardian of the Nile
2.	Frogs (8:1–15)	Given to Pharaoh (8:1–4)	"Covered the land of Egypt" (8:6b)	Dealt deceitfully, hardened his heart, refused to listen (8:8, 15)	Heqet—goddess of birth, with a frog head
3.	Gnats (or mosquitoes) (8:16–19)	None given	"All the land of Egypt" (8:17b)	Hardened his heart, refused to listen (8:19b)	Set—god of the desert
4.	Insects (or flies) (8:20–32)	Given to Pharaoh (8:20–23)	"All the land of Egypt," except Goshen (8:22, 24b)	Dealt deceitfully, hardened his heart, refused to release the Hebrews (8:25–29, 32)	Re—a sun god Uatchit—a god possibly represented by the fly
5.	Livestock epidemic (9:1–7)	Given to Pharaoh (9:1–5)	"All the livestock of Egypt died," but none of the Hebrews' died (9:6)	Hardened his heart, refused to release the Hebrews (9:7b)	Hathor—goddess with a cow head Apis—the bull god, symbol of fertility Mnevis—sacred bull of Heliopolis
6.	Boils (9:8–12)	None given	"'On man and beast through all the land of Egypt'" (9:9b)	God hardened his heart, refused to listen (9:12)	Sekhmet—goddess with power over disease Sunu—the pestilence god Isis—goddess of healing

Plagues	Warnings	Extent	Pharaoh's Responses	Egyptian Deities Most Likely Targeted by the Plagues
7. Hailstorm (9:13–35)	Given to Pharaoh (9:13–19)	"All the land of Egypt," except Goshen (9:25–26)	Dealt deceitfully, hardened his heart, refused to release the Hebrews (9:27–29, 34–35)	Nut—a sky goddess Osiris—god of crops and fertility Set—god of storms Seth—protector of crops
8. Locusts (10:1–20)	Given to Pharaoh (10:1–6)	"All the land of Egypt" (10:14a)	Dealt deceitfully, God hardened his heart, refused to release the Hebrews (10:16–17, 20)	Nut—a sky goddess Osiris—god of crops and fertility Seth—protector of crops
9. Darkness (10:21–29)	None given	"All the land of Egypt, except for all the sons of Israel" (10:22–23)	Dealt deceitfully, God hardened his heart, refused to release the Hebrews, told Moses to leave (10:24–28)	Re, Aten, Atum, Horus—all sun gods Nut, Hathor—sky goddesses
10. Death of the first-borns (11:1–12:32)	Given to Pharaoh (11:4–8)	"All the firstborn in the land of Egypt," but none of the Hebrews (11:6; 12:29a)	Told Moses and Aaron to lead the Hebrews with their possessions out of Egypt (12:31–32)	Min—god of reproduction Isis— goddess who protected children Heqet—goddess of birth Pharaoh's firstborn son—a god

Sources: The material on Egyptian deities given in this chart was drawn from John D. Hannah, "Exodus," in *The Bible Knowledge Commentary*, Old Testament ed., John F. Walvoord and Roy B. Zuck (Wheaton, Ill.: Scripture Press Publications, Victor Books, 1985).p. 120; John H. Walton, *Chronological and Background Charts of the Old Testament* (Grand Rapids, Mich.: Zondervan Publishing House, Academie Books, 1978), p. 43; and John J. Davis, *Moses and the Gods of Egypt: Studies in the Book of Exodus* (Grand Rapids, Mich.: Baker Book House, 1971), pp. 79–152.

Chapter 11

THE NIGHT NOBODY SLEPT

Exodus 11–12

In the last chapter, we watched as God judged the Egyptians with nine devastating plagues. While the Egyptians' spirits were breaking, their relentless Pharaoh stubbornly refused to let the Hebrews go.

A judgment even more severe will come soon, however. As we'll see in Exodus 11 and 12, God was preparing His tenth and final plague. His arrow of wrath was set on the string. His strong arm of justice was bending the bow and aiming the arrow at Egypt's firstborn. Only His mercy had prevented the deadly arrow from taking flight for this long. But the time had come for Him to set His people free. And the price for that freedom would be the death of countless Egyptians.

The Prediction: A Plague of Sorrow

When the thick darkness of the ninth plague dissipated after the third day, Pharaoh once again reconsidered, then rejected, Moses' demand to release the Hebrews and their possessions (Exod. 10:21–26). So God sent Moses to Pharaoh with one final message.

Announced to Moses

Knowing this final plague would secure the release of His people, God instructed Moses to prepare for the Exodus.

> Now the Lord said to Moses, "One more plague I will bring on Pharaoh and on Egypt; after that he will let you go from here. When he lets you go, he will surely drive you out from here completely. Speak now in the hearing of the people that each man ask from his neighbor and each woman from her neighbor for articles of silver and articles of gold." (11:1–2)

Why would the Hebrews need silver and gold? Wouldn't food and water be the logical supplies for a desert journey? The command to take precious articles, odd as it was, would eventually provide the people with the supplies they needed to build the tabernacle at Sinai. And the absence of food and water from God's list would give Him the opportunity to show His people that He could provide for their needs.

Received by Israel

Then "the Lord gave the [Hebrew] people favor in the sight of the Egyptians," and Moses became "greatly esteemed . . . both in the sight of Pharaoh's servants and in the sight of the people" (v. 3). Everyone, it seems, was listening to Moses and acting favorably toward the Hebrews. Everyone, that is, but Pharaoh.

Heard and Rejected by Pharaoh

Now came the time for Moses to announce God's next judgment to Pharaoh.[1]

> Moses said, "Thus says the Lord, 'About midnight I am going out into the midst of Egypt, and all the firstborn in the land of Egypt shall die, from the firstborn of the Pharaoh who sits on his throne, even to the firstborn of the slave girl who is behind the millstones; all the firstborn of the cattle as well.'"
> (vv. 4–5)

This wave of death would cause unprecedented sorrow in all the homes of Egypt (v. 6). The households of the Israelites, however, would not be touched (v. 7). God would pry the Israelites from Pharaoh's grip, distinguishing His chosen people from the Egyptians. The prospect of such widespread death—all because of Pharaoh's stubbornness—caused Moses to leave the king's presence "in hot anger" (v. 8).

But, as God assured Moses, Pharaoh's stubbornness would be the very thing He would use to show His power.

> Then the Lord said to Moses, "Pharaoh will not listen to you, so that My wonders will be multiplied in the land of Egypt." (v. 9)

Moses and Aaron had performed sign after sign, and Pharaoh

---

1. The first three verses in Exodus 11 stand as a parenthesis between 10:29 and 11:4. The confrontation between Moses and Pharaoh in 11:4–8 is not a separate event from the one in 10:24–29. Rather, they comprise one discussion that is interrupted by the parenthesis in 11:1–3. Consequently, Moses was still correct in saying that he and Pharaoh would never see each other again.

still had not relented (v. 10). The stage was set for God to release his wrath and end 430 years of slavery. There was only one more preparation to make.

The Memorial: The Passover Meal

Exodus 12 covers the Passover and the Exodus. You might expect, after 430 years of slavery, that Moses, the author of the book of Exodus, would spend a great deal of time on the Exodus itself—the details of organizing and mobilizing two million Hebrews,[2] a long-running narrative on the mass of humanity pouring out of Egypt into the wilderness, and so on. You might even expect him to spend some time depicting the graphic death of Egypt's firstborn, God's just judgment on an oppressive leader and nation.

Surprisingly, though, Moses dedicates very little of chapter 12 to these two events. He devotes most of it to the details of the Passover—its first observance and its continuing importance in the life of Israel. It would become a solemn ceremony regularly observed by the Israelites, keeping the high cost of their deliverance ever before them. So important was this Passover, it would mark the beginning of the religious year for them.

> "This month shall be the beginning of months for
> you; it is to be the first month of the year to you."
> (12:2)

Some Details to Observe

To prepare themselves for God's visitation of judgment upon Egypt, each Hebrew household, or group of households, was to choose one lamb on the tenth day of the first month (vv. 3–4).[3] The lambs were to be unblemished, one-year-old males (v. 5a). On the fourteenth day of the same month, all of the Israelites were to kill these special lambs at the twilight hour (v. 6). Some of the

---

2. Although we are not given an exact count, many Bible scholars estimate that the number of men, women, and children who left in the Exodus was more than two million. John J. Davis provides the reasoning behind this conclusion: "The number of men over twenty years of age is listed as 600,000. . . . Assuming that males over twenty constitute approximately one-fourth the population, the total number of Israelites involved in the exodus would have surpassed 2,000,000 people." *Moses and the Gods of Egypt: Studies in the Book of Exodus* (Grand Rapids, Mich.: Baker Book House, 1971), pp. 146.

3. This would have been the month of Abib, later called Nisan, which corresponds to our March–April.

blood that spilled from the carcasses was to be put on the two doorposts and lintels of each Israelite home where the meal was going to be eaten (v. 7).

That same evening the lamb was to be roasted and completely eaten, with unleavened bread and bitter herbs as side dishes (vv. 8–10). The Hebrews were to eat the meal quickly and be ready for travel with their sandals on their feet and their staffs in hand (v. 11). But why did they need to go through all this trouble? Wouldn't it be nicer just to lean back, enjoy a relaxing meal, and relish the thought of their approaching freedom? There was more going on here than just a meal. This was God's plan for saving the Jews from His wrath and securing their freedom.

> "'For I will go through the land of Egypt on that night, and will strike down all the firstborn in the land of Egypt, both man and beast; and against all the gods of Egypt I will execute judgments—I am the Lord. The blood shall be a sign for you on the houses where you live; and when I see the blood I will pass over you, and no plague will befall you to destroy you when I strike the land of Egypt.'" (vv. 12–13)

Every element of the Passover meal had a symbolic meaning and purpose, as commentator John D. Hannah explains.

> The slaying of the animals (instead of the Israelites' firstborn sons, v. 13) and the sprinkling of blood prefigured the substitutionary death of Christ. He is "our Passover Lamb" (1 Cor. 5:7), "a Lamb without blemish or defect" (1 Peter 1:19; cf. John 1:29). His own sacrifice is the means whereby individual believers escape the horrors of spiritual death.
>
> Bitter herbs . . . symbolized sorrow or grief (cf. Lam. 3:15) for past sin, or the Israelites' bitter experience of oppression in Egypt. The bread without yeast symbolized their leaving in haste (Ex. 12:11, 39; Deut. 16:3). The meat was to be roasted, not eaten raw as some pagans did. The people were to eat the entire meal quickly while dressed ready for travel. . . .
>
> Thus under the protection of shed blood, the congregation was to be reminded of cleansing from

sin (cf. Heb. 9:22) and that they were sojourners in a strange land.[4]

An Event to Remember

The rite of Passover was designed to be celebrated from generation to generation (Exod. 12:14 – 27, 42–51). The Jews were never to forget this day and what it represented.

> "And when your children say to you, 'What does this rite mean to you?' you shall say, 'It is a Passover sacrifice to the Lord who passed over the houses of the sons of Israel in Egypt when He smote the Egyptians, but spared our homes.'" (vv. 26–27a)

Moses leaned down so that Abiah could see the lamb he was holding in his arms. He had come to the girl's house to observe the Passover with her and her mother. The ten-year-old had lost her father less than a month ago, when an Egyptian overseer beat him to death because he failed to make his quota of bricks. Moses was here to comfort them and help them perform the rite of Passover.

"Abbi," he said to the girl, "put your hand on its forehead." Moses took her hand in his and placed it above the lamb's eyes. "Mariah, you too." The girl's mother stepped forward and placed her hand next to Abbi's. "Let's pray," he said.

As the two bowed their heads, Moses glanced up and looked toward the west. He saw the bright slice of sun setting behind the war monuments in the treasure city of Raamses. It looked like a flat,

4. John D. Hannah, "Exodus," in *The Bible Knowledge Commentary*, Old Testament edition, ed. John F. Walvoord and Roy B. Zuck (Wheaton, Ill.: Scripture Press Publications, Victor Books, 1985), p. 128.

red wafer descending in a wine-colored sky. The Lord's angel would be here soon.

"Lord," he said, "we offer this lamb as a sacrifice to you according to your command. Use it, its body and blood, to deliver us from the angel of death. Now, O Lord, come quickly. Amen."

The other two repeated Moses' "Amen" and watched him as he placed the animal in a shallow wood basin. Moses dug his fingers into the lamb's thick wool at the base of the neck. With one hand clenched tightly into the pelt, he drew a knife with the other. The dagger was one that he had received from a rich Egyptian family—one of the many fine articles they had given him as a result of God's decree. As he gripped the gold handle and raised the knife, shards of light danced on the silver blade. With one swift jerk, he cut deep into the neck.

Blood gushed from the wound and into the basin. The lamb jolted, quivered, then fell limp. Moses loosened his grip. After washing the blood from his hands, he knelt beside Abbi, who was struggling to understand this gruesome ceremony.

"I know, child. It's not a pretty sight," he said in a soft tone. "But the price of deliverance is high. The Egyptians will lose their firstborn tonight, but you and I will be spared because of the blood of this lamb."

The Response of the Hebrews

When the Israelites heard what the Lord wanted them to do and why, they bowed low and worshiped Him (v. 27b). Then they went and did all that the Lord had commanded Moses and Aaron

(v. 28). Now that they knew and understood God's will, they responded in obedience. And it was a good thing, too, for God's arrow of death was on its way to Egypt.

The Fulfillment: Death of the Firstborns

At the stroke of midnight, God struck the Egyptians as He had promised.

> Now it came about at midnight that the Lord struck all the firstborn in the land of Egypt, from the firstborn of Pharaoh who sat on his throne to the firstborn of the captive who was in the dungeon, and all the firstborn of cattle. (v. 29)

Once the Egyptians realized what had happened, a great cry arose "for there was no [Egyptian] home where there was not someone dead" (v. 30). And Pharaoh responded according to God's plan.

> Then he called for Moses and Aaron at night and said, "Rise up, get out from among my people, both you and the sons of Israel; and go, worship the Lord, as you have said. Take both your flocks and your herds, as you have said, and go, and bless me also." (vv. 31–32)

The Exodus: Freedom for the Hebrews

And so they went.

> And at the end of the four hundred and thirty years, to the very day, all the hosts of the Lord went out from the land of Egypt. (v. 41)

God's people departed with the wealth of Egypt (vv. 35–36) and "journeyed from Rameses to Succoth" (v. 37). They were accompanied by a "mixed multitude" of possibly other Semites and some native Egyptians as well as their flocks, herds, and other livestock (v. 38). God certainly "brought forth His people with joy" (Ps. 105:43).

What a miraculous day! God shook the Hebrews loose from Pharaoh's mighty hand. The Lord's deliverance, memorialized in the Passover, had arrived. Now the people could begin their walk into freedom . . . and a life lived fully for the One who had freed them.

Your Life: Slavery or Freedom?

Where are you spiritually? Are you still in Egypt or are you on your way to the Promised Land? The Bible teaches that if you haven't been freed by Christ, you're still a slave to sin (compare Rom. 6:6–7, 17). Christ is our Passover (1 Cor. 5:7), and Jesus accomplished what the sacrificial lambs of the Old Testament only pictured. He took away our sin (John 1:29). And He still takes away sin. The only way you can be freed from the shackles that bind you is to trust in Him for the forgiveness of your sins.

If you are already a child of God, this chapter holds a lesson for you, too. Just as the Hebrews were never to forget what God had done for them, we must never forget what Christ has done for us. That's why we have the Lord's Supper. This ordinance keeps the power and presence of God ever before us.

Furthermore, both the Passover and the Exodus remind us that we need to live in a perpetual state of readiness to respond to God's special call on our lives. The Israelites were willing and ready to move from the familiar to the unfamiliar at the moment God told them to go. We often forget that most of the slaves probably had never left Goshen. It was all they had ever known. We should be just as prepared as they were to change locations, jobs, or even careers if the Lord calls on us to do so. Are you ready? Will you be obedient when He calls?

 Living Insights

"Never look back."

While that may be good advice in some situations, it's not so good for the spiritual life. Part of moving ahead spiritually is looking back—remembering what Christ has done for us.

The same was true for the ancient Hebrews. Though they moved ahead into freedom, they were never to forget what God had done in the past.

> "You shall tell your son on that day, saying, 'It is because of what the Lord did for me when I came out of Egypt.' And it shall serve as a sign to you on your hand, and as a reminder on your forehead, that the law of the Lord may be in your mouth; for with a powerful hand the Lord brought you out of Egypt.

Therefore, you shall keep this ordinance at its appointed time from year to year." (Exod. 13:8–10)

Remembrance plays a powerful role in our spiritual journey. If we regularly remember and commemorate our own spiritual deliverance, we will relish the freedom in which we now walk.

To fully live for our Deliverer, we must always remember our deliverance. That's why God instituted the Passover, and that's why we observe the Lord's Table, Communion. At His table, we not only remember the giving of His body and blood for us, we also bask in the joyful reality of His present ministry—that of our intercessor and high priest.

When's the last time you took Communion, and what did it mean to you?

_____

_____

_____

_____

_____

How has your study of the Passover enriched your understanding of the Lord's Supper?

_____

_____

_____

_____

What other ideas (journaling, prayer, etc.) do you have for remembering the Lord's faithfulness in your life?

_____

_____

_____

_____

Chapter 12

BETWEEN THE DEVIL AND THE DEEP RED SEA
Exodus 14

Predicaments. We all face them. And we all have ways of describing them.

A cook, for example, might describe herself as being "in a pinch," "in a pickle," or "in a jam," whereas a baseball player might say he's "in a tight squeeze." Whether someone's "up a tree," "in a corner," "hard-pressed," "between a rock and a hard place," or "behind the eight ball," we all understand the situation. Whatever the expression, the meaning is the same—someone is facing trouble that cannot be easily escaped. Predicaments are uncomfortable, nerve-racking, and often threaten to drive us into despair.

Predicaments range from the personal to the global. Maybe you remember the Cuban Missile crisis of the early sixties, when the whole world teetered on the edge of nuclear war. Or what about the Iranian hostage dilemma of 1979–80?

Predicaments also abound in church history. Martin Luther, for example, was ordered to recant his teachings before the council at Worms . . . or become the established church's most hated enemy.

The Bible, too, is brimming with quandaries. Eve's moment of decision when tempted by the serpent in the garden . . . Jesus in Gethsemane, wrestling with the imminence of the Cross . . . and Moses and the Israelites, caught between the Red Sea and Pharaoh's pursuing army.

Let's look at Exodus 14 to see how God's people faced that predicament, and observe the desperation and dependence they displayed.

The Lord's Plan

By leading the Hebrews into the desert, Moses took the reins of a nation of people who had been surrounded by an Egyptian world view—philosophies, practices, and moral standards reflective of a godless society. Now God had called out His people to be distinct. He would write His Law—His standards of righteousness —on stone, engrave it in their hearts and minds, and require them to live for Him.

But before He could plant them in their new life, he had to uproot them from the old. That meant, in part, teaching them how to completely trust Him in the midst of seemingly hopeless predicaments.

> Now the Lord spoke to Moses, saying, "Tell the sons of Israel to turn back and camp before Pi-ha-hiroth, between Migdol and the sea; you shall camp in front of Baal-zephon, opposite it, by the sea." (Exod. 14:1–2)

At this location, they would see several massive Egyptian fortresses to the north, the barren Egyptian desert to the south, the deep Red Sea[1] to the east, the approaching Egyptian army to the west. In other words, God led His people into a geographic cul-de-sac—militarily, the most vulnerable spot they could have chosen.

The Egyptians' Pursuit

With the Hebrews nearing Egypt's borders and apparently either lost or severely disoriented, Pharaoh, his heart hardened by the Lord, reevaluated his decision to let them go.

> Pharaoh and his servants had a change of heart toward the people, and they said, "What is this we have done, that we have let Israel go from serving us?" (v. 5)

Pharaoh immediately set out after the Israelites, taking with him "six hundred select chariots, and all the other chariots of Egypt with officers over all of them" (vv. 6–7). This raging army rose over the Egyptian horizon, dust from its horses and chariots billowing into the sky. And all that the Hebrews could do was watch them come.

---

1. The Hebrew term *yam sûph* is often translated "Red Sea" (Exod. 13:18). Many contemporary Bible scholars, however, understand the word to mean "the Sea of Reeds." From this translation, some argue that Israel didn't cross a deep sea but a shallow swamp. Though the exact location of the crossing can't be determined for certain, the Bible is clear that the water was deep enough to cover and drown the Egyptian army. For more details on the identification of the "Red Sea," see John J. Davis, *Moses and the Gods of Egypt: Studies in the Book of Exodus* (Grand Rapids, Mich.: Baker Book House, 1971), pp. 168–71; Leon Wood, *A Survey of Israel's History* (Grand Rapids, Mich.: Zondervan Publishing House, 1970), pp. 129–30; and John Rea, "Exodus, The," in the *Wycliffe Bible Encyclopedia*, ed. Charles F. Pfeiffer, Howard F. Vos, and John Rea (Chicago, Ill.: Moody Press, 1975), pp. 571–72.

The Hebrews' Panic

The sight of the approaching Egyptian army struck fear in the hearts of the Hebrews (v. 10a). Their first response was to cry out to the Lord to rescue them (v. 10b). But then they blamed Moses for getting them into this fix. Listen to their stinging and ungrateful words.

> "Is it because there were no graves in Egypt that you have taken us away to die in the wilderness? Why have you dealt with us in this way, bringing us out of Egypt? Is this not the word that we spoke to you in Egypt, saying, 'Leave us alone that we may serve the Egyptians'? For it would have been better for us to serve the Egyptians than to die in the wilderness." (vv. 11–12)

With Pharaoh's army bearing down on him from one direction and his people's jabbing accusations coming from the other, Moses stood tall—and called on the name of the Lord.

> But Moses said to the people, "Do not fear! Stand by and see the salvation of the Lord which He will accomplish for you today; for the Egyptians whom you have seen today, you will never see them again forever. The Lord will fight for you while you keep silent." (vv. 13–14)

Instead of defending himself against the people's accusations, Moses confidently directed their attention to their delivering God.

Did you notice what Moses wanted the people to do? "Do not fear." "Stand by." "See." "Keep silent." These are all responses that demonstrate our trust in God during predicaments.

Unfortunately, though, those four commands rub against the grain of our natural instincts. When Pharaoh's army bears down on us, we often fear the worst, rush right into the fight, look to ourselves instead of God, or try to talk our way out of things. But God wants us to do the exact opposite. He wants us to show confidence in Him, face our dilemma, watch Him work, and keep quiet as He delivers us.

The Lord's Protection

With their backs against the sea and the world's most powerful army charging closer and closer, God once again worked through His servant Moses to miraculously deliver His people.

> The angel of God, who had been going before the camp of Israel, moved and went behind them; and the pillar of cloud moved from before them and stood behind them. So it came between the camp of Egypt and the camp of Israel; and there was the cloud along with the darkness, yet it gave light at night. Thus the one did not come near the other all night. (vv. 19–20)

What an amazing sight that must have been! The pillars of fire and cloud that were leading the people out of Egypt turned, flew over their heads, and landed squarely between them and the Egyptians. The charging warriors couldn't advance any further. The God of heaven stood in their way.

> Then Moses stretched out his hand over the sea; and the Lord swept the sea back by a strong east wind all night and turned the sea into dry land, so the waters were divided. (v. 21)

Many people skim over that verse, and assume that the Hebrews walked onto the sea bed as soon as the waters parted. But that's not how it happened. They watched all night as God sent a powerful wind to dry up the muddy bottom. It must have been difficult for the people to choose between watching the pillar of fire hold off the Egyptians or watching the wind blow a dry path through the sea! There was, however, no difficult choice about what to do when morning came.

> The sons of Israel went through the midst of the sea on the dry land, and the waters were like a wall to them on their right hand and on their left. (v. 22)

When Pharaoh saw the Hebrews escaping, he resumed his pursuit, chasing them "into the midst of the sea" (v. 23). As the army drew closer, the Lord tripped them up by causing "their chariot wheels to swerve, and He made them drive with difficulty; so the Egyptians said, 'Let us flee from Israel, for the Lord is fighting for them against the Egyptians'" (v. 25). What happened next marks one of the greatest events of deliverance in the Old Testament.

Then the Lord said to Moses, "Stretch out your hand over the sea so that the waters may come back over the Egyptians, over their chariots and their horsemen." So Moses stretched out his hand over the sea, and the sea returned to its normal state at daybreak, while the Egyptians were fleeing right into it; then the Lord overthrew the Egyptians in the midst of the sea. The waters returned and covered the chariots and the horsemen, even Pharaoh's entire army that had gone into the sea after them; not even one of them remained. (vv. 26–28)

*T*hey're coming, Moses! Hurry!" Aaron shouted from the edge of the sea.

Moses was the last of the Hebrews still below the water line, and he was climbing up the steep bank. The first line of Egyptian chariots was thundering across the dry strip and gaining on him quickly. They would overtake him in only moments.

"Faster, Moses! Faster! Don't look back. Just climb!"

The warriors in the first row of chariots pulled arrows from their quivers. In unison they strung their bows and hoisted the loaded weapons into the air. More than a dozen deadly arrows were aimed at Moses' back.

"Help us, Lord!" Aaron cried.

Then something went wrong. One chariot jolted and shook. Its archer lost his footing, fell down and tumbled out the back. The unmanned chariot swerved to the right and careened into the next carriage, clipping the leg of the horse pulling it. Both chariots locked together into a deadly ball and somersaulted into the rest of the row. The few arrows that left their bows flew indiscriminately into the sky or into the walls of water on either side.

The second row of warriors, consisting of mounted soldiers, pulled to a halt. The dust from the wreckage billowed into a thick cloud, but the commander pressed on. He raised his spear to signal the advance.

"Chaaaarge!" he bellowed, and bolted forward through the dust. But the other soldiers held back. The commander and his mount rushed blindly ahead. He thrust his spear out front as the horse's hoofs thundered and its nostrils flared and snorted. They sliced deep into the cloud and almost disappeared. Then the mount jerked to a stop, flipping the commander over its head. The animal's legs folded, but it didn't fall to the ground; it was propped up by a large pulling beam impaled through its chest.

The third-row commander kicked his horse forward and yelled at the second-row soldiers, "Charge!"

"Their god!" a soldier answered. "He's fighting for them."

"Retreat! Retreat!" the commander ordered as he pointed his spear back towards the bank they had come from.

The horsemen turned their mounts, and the foot soldiers ran toward the bank they had just left. The remaining chariots slammed into each other as they tried to flee. The second-row commander turned and watched the last Hebrew clear the water line. Then, the walls of water that had stood so solid looked like they were starting to melt . . . and come down in a drowning torrent.

The Hebrews' Praise

Isn't it amazing what God can do without our help? Sometimes we feel like our efforts are so vital to His plan that He can't go on without us. But it's His power, not ours, that sees us through. And sometimes we need to be reminded of that. When He does remind us, all we can do, like the Hebrews, is believe in Him all the more.

> When Israel saw the great power which the Lord had used against the Egyptians, the people feared the Lord, and they believed in the Lord and in His servant Moses. (v. 31)

It must have been a sobering sight to watch the bodies of those strong Egyptian soldiers lapping onto shore, facedown. What a reminder to the Hebrews that they could have never escaped without the Lord's intervention! They had seen His power. Now they sang His praises:

> "I will sing to the Lord, for He is highly exalted;
> The horse and its rider He has hurled into the sea.
> The Lord is my strength and song,
> And He has become my salvation;
> This is my God, and I will praise Him:
> My father's God, and I will extol Him." (15:1–2)

Our "Red Sea" Experiences

This account was not recorded simply for our amazement. Like the rest of the Bible, it "was written for our instruction, that through perseverance and the encouragement of the Scriptures we might have hope" (Rom. 15:4b). Given this fact, let's consider four timeless principles suggested in Exodus 14.

First, *it takes tight places to break lifetime habits.* Some of our sinful thoughts, words, or actions have become so entrenched that we need to be placed in a spiritual cul-de-sac where we must face and deal with them.

Second, *when hemmed in on all sides, the only place to look is up.* It's amazing how times of intense pressure can help us look beyond ourselves and put our trust in God. Those times tend to reduce our selfishness and increase our teachability.

Third, *if the Lord is to get the glory, then He must do the fighting.* When we hit those threatening impasses, we often panic and try to run. However, there's a better approach. We might say it like this: "When I wait, He fights; when He fights, He wins; when He wins, I learn." The only sure way to honor God and grow through a predicament is to turn the situation over to Him. Once we do, we should stay out of His way and watch Him work.

Fourth, *"Red Seas" open and close at the Lord's command, no one else's.* God is not tied to our time schedules. He'll deliver us from our predicaments, but according to His purposes for our lives.

 Living Insights

"On the horns of a dilemma," "back against the wall," "up a creek without a paddle"—no matter how you say it, it's no fun being in a situation that has no apparent way out. Picking up on our four applications, answer the following questions, reflecting on how God uses difficult situations in your life to mold you into His image.

It takes tight places to break lifetime habits. What are some of the "tight places" you've experienced?

_____

_____

_____

Did God use these to break any habits and bring you to trust Him more? How?

_____

_____

_____

When hemmed in on all sides, the only place to look is up. When have you been hemmed in on all sides?

_____

_____

_____

What new qualities did God mold into your life as a result?

_____

_____

_____

If the Lord is to get the glory, then He must do the fighting. Why do we tend to take our battles into our own hands?

_____

_____

_____

How has God become victorious in your life apart from your efforts?

_____

_____

_____

_____

"Red Seas" open and close at the Lord's command, no one else's. When have you questioned God's timing in your life?

_____

_____

_____

What lessons did you learn as a result of His perfect timing?

_____

_____

_____

_____

Chapter 13

A HEAVENLY DIET VERSUS AN EARTHLY APPETITE

Exodus 16–17

Ⅰt's an acquired taste."

That's what my mom told me the first time I tried liver and onions. Now, you might be thinking, *Not in a million years.* Maybe liver and onions never became an appetizing dish for you. For me, however, my mom ended up being right. Now that I'm an adult, I occasionally do enjoy a serving of chicken-fried beef liver with sautéed onions—as long as my wife is planning to spend the next several days out of my breathing distance . . . say, in the next state.

How about you? Can you identify at least one food you hated as a child but grew up to enjoy? Was it spinach? Collard greens? Onions? Tomatoes? Whatever the food, it was probably good for you. In general, it takes much longer to acquire a taste for healthy food than it does for sweets and junk food.

The same is true for spiritual "food." Trusting God to provide all that we need for our spiritual life is an "acquired taste." It doesn't always come naturally. We often take the fast-food approach to the spiritual life—trusting in our limited perspective, depending on our exhaustible resources, relying on our own strength—instead of trusting in our all-sufficient God.

That's why God leads us into situations that bring us to the end of ourselves—so that we will lose our craving for self-sufficiency and learn to feast upon the bounty that He provides. Observing how He provided both physical and spiritual food for the ancient Hebrews just may help us trust Him more completely today.

A Song by the Sea

Before we consider how God transformed the Hebrews' spiritual appetite, let's get our bearings on their location and condition.

We just came from the scene in which the Lord delivered His children at the Red Sea. Following that miraculous event, the Hebrews "feared the Lord, and they believed in the Lord and in His servant Moses" (Exod. 14:31b). Then the people, gathered on the banks of the sea, began to sing.

> "I will sing to the Lord, for He is highly exalted;
> The horse and its rider He has hurled into the sea.
> The Lord is my strength and song,
> And He has become my salvation;
> This is my God, and I will praise Him;
> My father's God, and I will extol Him.
> The Lord is a warrior;
> The Lord is His name.
> Pharaoh's chariots and his army He has cast into
>   the sea;
> And the choicest of the officers are drowned in
>   the Red Sea." (15:1–4)

The Hebrews' song of praise continues for another fourteen verses, describing the Lord's might and His love for His children. Then, as the excitement begins to crest and the praise crescendos into exuberance, Miriam takes the timbrel and leads all the women in a dance and chorus.

> "Sing to the Lord, for He is highly exalted;
> The horse and his rider He has hurled into the sea."
> (v. 21)

What a day of rejoicing for God's people! But would their joy—as well as their praise and trust—continue as they moved from miraculous deliverance to the daily grind of depending on God for sustenance? We'll see. For as soon as the song was over, "Moses led Israel from the Red Sea, and they went out into the wilderness of Shur" (v. 22a).

Dependence in the Desert

The Desert of Shur was a barren region stretching eastward from Egypt to the Sinai Peninsula—where Moses would take the people to receive the Ten Commandments. Even today, this area is a wasteland, devoid of any vegetation except near springs and wells.

Isn't that a perfect parallel to the Christian walk? At conversion, we go through a Red Sea experience. We pass from impending death to a new life. Through our faith in Jesus Christ, God unlocks the shackles of our slavery to sin and escorts us to a fresh start. It's a wonderful time. But becoming a Christian doesn't remove all of life's difficulties. Between the Red Sea and the Promised Land is the wilderness.

God didn't whisk the Hebrews from the Red Sea to the Promised Land, and he certainly doesn't whisk us straight to heaven the moment we're saved. Instead, he sends us on a long sojourn through a world that presents us with all kinds of opportunities to trust (or not trust) Him. We often fluctuate between enjoying the abundance He provides and complaining that He's given us too little. So how did the Hebrews respond to their trek through the wilderness? Let's find out.

Where's the Water?

> And they went three days in the wilderness and found no water. When they came to Marah, they could not drink the waters of Marah, for they were bitter; therefore it was named Marah. (vv. 22b–23)

In the heat of the desert, with no water in sight—except the undrinkable water of Marah—abundance and expectation melted into disappointment. And disappointment gave way to complaining.

> So the people grumbled at Moses, saying, "What shall we drink?" (v. 24)

Can you believe it? The Hebrews turned on their leader—only three days after seeing God perform a miracle with water. Couldn't a God who parted the Red Sea supply water to drink? How quickly they (and we) forget.

Moses, the intercessor, cried out to the Lord for help, and God made the bitter waters sweet (v. 25). He provided. But not before He had tested them (v. 25b). The wilderness is a place of testing. Deuteronomy 8:2, though it refers to a later and longer wilderness wandering, helps us understand why the wilderness is part of God's plan for us.

> "You shall remember all the way which the Lord your God has led you in the wilderness these forty years, that He might humble you, testing you, to know what was in your heart, whether you would keep His commandments or not."

The wilderness shows us what we're made of. Shows us what's

in our hearts. Shows us whether our spiritual tastes tend toward the earthly or heavenly. In the wilderness, our total dependency and God's total sufficiency come together. In the wilderness, we grow.

God used this instance of the Israelites' grumbling to remind them that obeying Him would bring blessing . . . and that disobedience would bring cursing (Exod. 15:26). Then he brought them to Elim, a place of refreshment and rest (v. 27). How good and gracious of God to provide once again exactly what they needed. How long, though, would the people remember His gifts?

Manna from Heaven

We don't know how long the people camped at Elim. But when they left, they traveled south toward Mount Sinai, arriving at the Wilderness of Sin exactly one month after they had left Egypt (16:1). When food supplies started to dwindle, the people once again grumbled about their circumstances instead of trusting God. This time they blamed both Moses and Aaron.

> The sons of Israel said to them, "Would that we had died by the Lord's hand in the land of Egypt, when we sat by the pots of meat, when we ate bread to the full; for you have brought us out into this wilderness to kill this whole assembly with hunger." (v. 3)

Amazing! Now they were wishing for the "good old days" back in Egypt. Their physical hunger pangs quelled their appetite for God. Had they forgotten that they were slaves in Egypt—human pack animals who either heeled to Pharaoh's commands or felt his whip across their backs? They were ready to trade their freedom . . . for food.

Yet, just as He had done at Marah, God met their grumbling not with anger or judgment, but with provision. With abundance. With grace. He gave them daily bread from heaven (vv. 4–7).

Not Only Bread, but Meat

God's bounteous provision didn't stop there. Though Moses and Aaron grew tired of the people's complaints, God continued to respond to the Israelites' grumblings with patience (vv. 8–12). And He, once again, miraculously supplied what they needed.

> So it came about at evening that the quails came up and covered the camp, and in the morning there

was a layer of dew around the camp. When the layer of dew evaporated, behold, on the surface of the wilderness there was a fine flake-like thing, fine as the frost on the ground. When the sons of Israel saw it, they said to one another, "What is it?" For they did not know what it was. And Moses said to them, "It is the bread which the Lord has given you to eat." (vv. 13–15)

Meat and bread. They would have returned to Egypt for these. But God fed them from His own hand, showing them that He was their sufficiency and their sustenance. God then gave the people instructions on how to gather the bread, and there was plenty to go around (vv. 16–18). They were to gather only enough for one day and trust Him for the next day's supply (v. 19). If they tried to hoard the bread, it turned foul (vv. 20–21).

The Provision of the Sabbath

The day before the Sabbath, the Israelites were to gather two-day's worth of bread. On the Sabbath, they were to rest. Some of the people, though—even after all they had seen God do—didn't trust Him to supply their needs. They went out on the Sabbath looking for a fresh crust of manna, finding none (vv. 22–30).

This sweet manna from heaven was to be more than a meal for this generation. It would be a memorial to future generations. God commanded Moses and Aaron to store some manna, so that the Israelites would never forget God's faithfulness and goodness to them (vv. 31–36).

Water from the Rock

Journeying from the wilderness of Sin, the Israelites arrived at Rephidim, northwest of Sinai. And once again, they found themselves without water (17:1). Certainly they would look to God to supply their needs now. He had slaked their thirst at Marah. He had stuffed their stomachs with quail and manna. Surely they were done complaining. Or were they?

Moses took his seat among the circle of elders. He looked around the tent; not one more person could have been packed in, sitting or standing. People stood along the tent walls, anticipating the confrontation about to take place.

Once again, the Israelites were without water. And once again, they blamed Moses. They were tired of not having what they wanted when they wanted it. It was time to take some action. The room buzzed with accusation and blame.

"Give us water that we may drink," they said to Moses.

"Why do you quarrel with me," Moses answered. "Why do you test the Lord?"

Their memories were as short as their tongues were parched. Though God had never failed to provide for them, their thirst for water burned away their trust in Him—and their confidence in Moses. "Why, now, have you brought us up from Egypt, to kill us and our children and our livestock with thirst?" they accused.

Several of the elders stood and pointed a finger at Moses. The shouting grew louder and meaner. And Moses feared for his life. He wondered when the people might stop hurling accusations . . . and start throwing stones.

Instead of allowing His servant to be killed with rocks, God led Moses to a rock of life.

"Behold, I will stand before you there on the rock at Horeb; and you shall strike the rock, and water will come out of it, that the people may drink." And

Moses did so in the sight of the elders of Israel. He named the place Massah and Meribah because of the quarrel of the sons of Israel, and because they tested the Lord, saying, "Is the Lord among us, or not?" (vv. 6–7)

He was among them indeed.

Military Victory

God not only filled the Israelites' stomachs and quenched their thirst, He gave them victory over the Amalekites, who apparently saw this huge nomadic nation of Hebrews as a threat to their security and attacked them. Once again, God used Moses in this miraculous provision (vv. 8–16).

Provision and Victory: Ours in Christ

The Hebrews' experiences are instructive for us for two reasons. First, they encourage us to practice the right things. To remain teachable and humble during hardship. To keep reminding ourselves of God's past faithfulness. To never let our earthly appetites squelch our desire for Him.

Second, the wanderings of the Israelites direct us to the right Person—Jesus Christ. Did you notice some of the images of Christ in these passages? Jesus gives us living water that brings eternal life (John 4:13–14). He is the bread that comes down from heaven (6:32). He is the Rock that was struck so that we might have life (1 Cor. 10:4). He has won the victory for us over sin and Satan (1 Cor. 15:56–57).

Jesus Christ is not only our deliverer from the slavery of sin; He is our sustainer, our provider, our champion as we sojourn in this wilderness on the way to heaven. He will take us through this life . . . and into the next.

 Living Insights

We, like the ancient Hebrews, often grumble when we think God has mistreated or forgotten us. When we focus too much on our lack of earthly provisions, we forget that God abundantly supplies all our physical and spiritual needs. To battle a grumbling spirit, we need to focus our minds on praise. Consider for a moment how

God has met your needs and made it possible for you to serve Him.
Recall the times in your past when God has provided for your
needs in both big and small ways.

_____

_____

_____

_____

Write down some of His wonderful attributes, such as His power
over creation, His patience with you, and His enduring love for His
people.

_____

_____

_____

Finally, express your confidence that the Lord will take care of
your needs and use you for His glory.

_____

_____

_____

Now, in light of God's past faithfulness, describe your current
problems and/or needs to Him—with the confidence that He
knows and meets all your needs.

_____

_____

_____

_____

Be sure and pack this away for the wilderness trek. . . . That
way you can refresh your memory now and then.

Chapter 14
WHY LEADERS CRACK UP
Exodus 18

Have you ever had to go to the Department of Motor Vehicles, perhaps to renew your driver's license or auto registration? If you have, you probably *had* to go—no one ever, never goes to the DMV voluntarily! What makes the trip there so dreaded? Why all the fuss about the DMV? The answer consists of two words that should never, ever go together: *long lines.*

Nothing squeezes the schedule and sucks the heart and soul out of a person more quickly and completely than the endless stream of bodies at the DMV. Long lines in other places are bad enough, but at least there's something to look forward to. At the movie theater, you'll probably see a good film. At the soup kitchen, you'll get a warm meal and a cold drink. But what awaits you at the DMV? A rude state employee and a horrid photograph that will haunt you for the next four years. "Smile." (FLASH!) "Now fill out this form, and go to window C . . ."

But step on the other side of the counter and view life through the eyes of a DMV employee. Face after face after face . . . the fearful, the cocky, the angry . . . crying babies, out-of-control kids, screaming parents . . . all wanting something *now*. The glares and not-so-under-the-breath remarks when it's time for a much-needed break make the endless line of people that much harder to bear. Too much to do. Too little time and too few people to do it. Pretty typical problem of our day. But definitely not a new one.

Moses rose from his prayers, walked to the tent flap, and paused. He needed just one more moment of solitude before facing the legion of Hebrews awaiting him. This day, like many before it and many more to come, would become a long, mind-numbing day of settling disputes among the people.

116

He stepped outside and descended the gentle slope from his tent to the court. Entering the waiting area, he passed through a sea of people all sitting on the ground in endless lines. At the far end, the Hebrews had constructed a wooden platform—a judgment seat for Moses' new role.

Ascending the platform, he stood in front of the makeshift judicial bench facing the people, who simultaneously rose up. "May the blessing of Yahweh rest on you," he said to the people. They raised their hands and responded, "Amen, amen." As a whole, they looked like twelve tributaries feeding into a single basin. Moses began to feel like he was drowning.

When he sat, the people followed his cue. With a sigh, Moses called the first case, and thus his endless day began.

You don't have to work at or visit the DMV to feel like Moses and the Israelites did. Our society is filled with workaholics, soccer moms, and stressed-out student leaders trying to do too much, too fast. Usually, we end up exhausted, frustrated, angry, and lonely.

Does God provide a solution to draining problems like this? Absolutely! Moses received God's guidance, and so can we, through the wise words of his father-in-law, Jethro. Let's join them in Exodus 18 to learn some practical ways to cope with the demands of leadership.

A Visit from Jethro

With Egypt far behind and Mount Sinai drawing closer, Moses struggled to keep pace with the demands of leading the Israelites as they camped in the wilderness. Then came a welcome visit—from his father-in-law, Jethro, who brought Moses' wife Zipporah and his two boys, Gershom and Eliezer (Exod. 18:2–6). What a wonderful family reunion it must have been! They were like a refreshing cool drink of water to this desert wanderer's soul.

Why had Jethro come? Of course, to reunite the family, but also because he had "heard of all that God had done for Moses and for Israel His people, how the Lord had brought Israel out of Egypt" (v. 1). When Moses saw him, "he bowed down and kissed him; and they asked each other of their welfare and went into the tent" (v. 7). Then the stories of Egypt began to flow.

> Moses told his father-in-law all that the Lord had done to Pharaoh and to the Egyptians for Israel's sake, all the hardship that had befallen them on the journey, and how the Lord had delivered them. (v. 8)

It must have been an eye-popping, jaw-dropping experience for the four visitors as they listened to Moses tell the wonders of the Lord's deliverance and provision. The reports moved their hearts so strongly that they held a worship service to commemorate His mighty deeds.

> Then Jethro, Moses' father-in-law, took a burnt offering and sacrifices for God, and Aaron came with all the elders of Israel to eat a meal with Moses' father-in-law before God. (v. 12)

An Evaluation of Moses

After the refreshing time with his family, Moses returned to another day of tiresome duties before the people.

Moses' Practice

> It came about the next day that Moses sat to judge the people, and the people stood about Moses from the morning until the evening. (v. 13)

Did you notice the length of Moses' workday? "Morning until the evening." He was staying at the office too long, overworking himself. When Jethro saw all the work and time Moses was putting in, he asked two simple, direct questions.

> "What is this thing that you are doing for the people? Why do you alone sit as judge and all the people stand about you from morning until evening?" (v. 14b)

First, Jethro asked Moses about his *priorities*: "Why, Moses, have you supplanted your primary role as the Israelites' leader with the lesser role of being their judge?" His second question related to *personnel*: "Why are you shouldering the burden of judging the people all by yourself, Moses?" Moses responded with a single, honest answer.

> "Because the people come to me to inquire of God. When they have a dispute, it comes to me, and I judge between a man and his neighbor, and make known the statutes of God and His laws." (vv. 15b–16)

Moses didn't see that anything was wrong. So he simply explained that his charge as the Hebrews' leader naturally included making judgments between them. It was an enormous job, and Moses was doing his best to fulfill his calling.

Fortunately, Jethro had a few helpful suggestions.

Jethro's Advice

Seeing the situation from the outside, Jethro was able to bring some greatly needed objectivity. He pointed out that the way Moses was performing his job would eventually lead to despair.

> "You will surely wear out, both yourself and these people who are with you, for the task is too heavy for you; you cannot do it alone."[1] (v. 18)

Moses already knew that his attempt to be a judge was exhausting, not only for him but for the long lines of people he saw every day. But what could he do? Jethro had two wise pieces of advice for him.

First, *represent the people before God and teach them His Word.* Jethro told Moses to reorganize his priorities.

> "Now listen to me: I will give you counsel, and God be with you. You be the people's representative before

---

1. "The task is too heavy for you; you cannot do it alone." Jethro's words to Moses were more than advice on how to delegate. They remind us that Moses' limitations point to God's all-sufficiency. Moses could lead the people to the Red Sea, but only God could get them across. Only God could make bitter water sweet, provide manna and quail, bring water gushing from a rock—not Moses, whom the people were constantly grumbling against. During the battle with the Amalekites, he grew weary and needed two people to hold up his arms. Judging the people, he grew overwhelmed and needed his father-in-law's wisdom and the help of many others. Only God is all-powerful and all-wise; and Moses, though a strong and faithful leader, had imperfections that only point to the need for our perfect Savior, the Lord Jesus Christ.

God, and you bring the disputes to God, then teach them the statutes and the laws, and make known to them the way in which they are to walk and the work they are to do." (vv. 19–20)

By returning to the primary role God had called him to, Moses could provide leadership for the whole group much better than he could when he was trying to address their needs individually.

Second, *delegate authority by choosing qualified men to help you lead the people*. Jethro gave Moses a plan for dividing up the responsibilities of judging the people.

"Furthermore, you shall select out of all the people able men who fear God, men of truth, those who hate dishonest gain; and you shall place these over them as leaders of thousands, of hundreds, of fifties and of tens. Let them judge the people at all times; and let it be that every major dispute they will bring to you, but every minor dispute they themselves will judge. So it will be easier for you, and they will bear the burden with you." (vv. 21–22)

Basically, Jethro told Moses to delegate his incidental responsibilities and retain his essential ones. If Moses would follow his father-in-law's counsel, he would be able to endure his job and the Israelites would find more peace (v. 23).

A Change in Method

Moses wisely chose to accept Jethro's advice, even to the letter: "Moses listened to his father-in-law and did all that he had said" (v. 24; see also vv. 25–26). With the new system of leadership in place, "Moses bade his father-in-law farewell, and he went his way into his own land" (v. 27).

Some Principles for Today

This chapter in Moses' life contains several valuable guidelines for us today, whether our job is to lead a corporation, care for our children, or do our homework.

First, *in every responsibility, two factors are present—the essential and the additional*. The essentials are the areas of our calling. No matter how hard we try or how much we want to, we can't wear fifty different hats. We need to do what we do best to the best of our abilities—and if it's possible, delegate the additionals. Even if that means giving tasks to others who will do them differently, or, heaven help us, less "perfectly" than we do them!

Second, *as the workload increases, wise leaders restrain their involvement and involve others more.* People who have held a leadership position in a company that has undergone a lot of growth find this principle especially difficult to apply. Many times, these leaders continue to operate with a method of leadership that can only be effective in an environment where the workload is light. But when the responsibilities increase, a person must adapt his or her leadership style and recruit gifted, capable people to help carry the burden of the additional load.

Third, *God's servants are not exempt from the penalties of breaking life's natural laws.* Failure to delegate sufficiently will inevitably lead to a physical, emotional, or mental breakdown. No one can continue functioning under intense pressure and long working hours without cracking in some way. That's how God has designed us. He never meant for us to tackle alone a task that requires more than one person to accomplish. So when we try to operate against His design, we actually violate His laws.

Fourth, *efficiency is increased not only by what is accomplished but also by what is relinquished.* Whenever we believe we can or should do it all and at the same time maintain a high standard of productivity and excellence, we should reflect long and hard on Moses' ineffective leadership methods. Not only did he exhaust himself, but he also failed to meet the numerous needs of his people. Moses, however, remedied his situation by applying Jethro's sound advice and relinquishing the additionals.

How about you? Are your responsibilities beginning to weigh on your shoulders, causing you to despise what God has charged you with instead of enjoying them? Maybe you've started to dread going to work or the kids are frazzling your nerves more than usual. Perhaps school has lost all interest for you, and you're wishing there were a way out. It could be that your feelings are the result of taking on too much responsibility. If so, take a quiet moment to listen to Jethro's advice. Identify your priorities, and then delegate the "additionals" to trustworthy people.

Living Insights

Many of us suffer from the problem of super-efficiency. We're unwilling to share the load with those around us, or maybe just afraid of letting go and losing control. Take a minute, though, to consider what you might lose if you continue to overburden yourself.

Your Distinctiveness

When we take on too many activities unrelated to the way God has gifted us, our gifts begin to suffer. We shift away from our priorities and lose direction and focus. As a result, our distinctive contribution gets blurred. Take a moment to list your gifts and the areas where they are best utilized.

_____

_____

_____

_____

Have you added any nonessentials that are diluting your gifts? If so, what are they?

_____

_____

_____

_____

Are you willing to let go of them? How can you begin releasing those add-ons and live more strongly in the distinctive way God made you?

_____

_____

_____

Your Family

If you're spending excess time at the office, you're spending less time with your spouse and children. If you're spending too much time running the children to and fro, you might be ignoring the most important relationship in your family—your marriage. List the people in your life, friends as well as family, who suffer when you take on too heavy a load.

_____

_____

_____

_____

_____

Now that you've considered the high cost of shouldering too much responsibility, write down all the duties you are currently handling in the following areas.

Family _____

_____

_____

_____

Work _____

_____

_____

Church _____

_____

_____

_____

Extracurricular Activities _____

_____

_____

_____

   Now, prioritize the above lists by circling the duties you consider to be essentials and drawing a box around the additionals. This moment, ask God to bring trustworthy people into your life to help you bear the burden of the additionals. Commit yourself to start delegating those responsibilities this week.

Chapter 15

SINAI: WHERE MOSES MET GOD

Exodus 19

With Jethro on his way home (Exod. 18:27), Moses and the Israelites packed up and left Rephidim for Sinai, where they would have a stunning encounter with their Redeemer and Lord. Entering God's presence would be no frivolous matter for the Hebrews. The chasm between His holiness and their depravity was too deep and wide to make Him easily accessible. So when they arrived at Sinai, God began preparing them to covenant with and worship Him.

As we listen to God's words and watch Moses and the people prepare to meet Him, let's also consider how we prepare to meet with God. Too often, whether at church or during our private devotions, we come into God's presence flippantly, not really aware of how awesome He is. This meeting at Sinai can revive our reverence—if we take these Scriptures to heart.

Gathering at Sinai

Just as God had promised Moses, way back before the deliverance from Egypt, he and the Hebrews would now worship the Lord together at Mount Sinai (Exod. 3:12).

> In the third month after the sons of Israel had gone out of the land of Egypt, on that very day they came into the wilderness of Sinai. When they set out from Rephidim, they came to the wilderness of Sinai and camped in the wilderness; and there Israel camped in front of the mountain. (19:1–2)

Three long months had passed since the Hebrews' miraculous exodus from Egypt. And for the next eleven months, here at Sinai they would stay (see Num. 10:11).[1] From these time frames alone,

---

1. Walter C. Kaiser Jr. points out that during this nearly yearlong time, "some fifty-eight chapters of Scripture (Exod 19–40; Lev 1–27; Num 1–10) were given here at Sinai." "Exodus," in *The Expositor's Bible Commentary*, gen. ed. Frank E. Gaebelein (Grand Rapids, Mich.: Zondervan Publishing House, Academic and Professional Books, 1990), vol. 2, p. 414.

we can see that God never rushes into His people's lives, nor do we quickly find His presence.

Once the two-million-plus Israelites were settled in camp, Moses made the arduous journey up the mountain to meet with God.

> Moses went up to God, and the Lord called to him from the mountain, saying, "Thus you shall say to the house of Jacob and tell the sons of Israel: 'You yourselves have seen what I did to the Egyptians, and how I bore you on eagles' wings, and brought you to Myself.'" (Exod. 19:3–4)

How tender the words of the Lord are. Eagles spread their wings underneath their fledglings to catch them as they learn to fly. In using this image, God says He safely carried and delivered His fledgling people out of Egypt and through the wilderness. His goal? To bring them to Himself. He always seeks us first, then waits for our response.

And a response was what He asked for next.

> "'If you will indeed obey My voice and keep My covenant, then you shall be My own possession among all the peoples, for all the earth is Mine; and you shall be to Me a kingdom of priests and a holy nation.'" (vv. 5–6a)

Specifically, God was looking for a willingness on the Hebrews' part to obey and be faithful to His covenant. If they would do this, then God promised them a special relationship and identity. Commentator John I. Durham elaborates.

> Israel as [God's "own possession"] is Israel become uniquely Yahweh's prized possession by their commitment to him in covenant. Israel as a "kingdom of priests" is Israel committed to the extension throughout the world of the ministry of Yahweh's Presence. . . . Israel as a "holy [nation]" . . . are to be a people set apart, different from all other people by what they are and are becoming—a display-people, a showcase to the world of how being in covenant with Yahweh changes a people.[2]

2. John I. Durham, *Exodus*, Word Biblical Commentary Series (Waco, Tex.: Word Books, Publisher, 1987), vol. 3, p. 263.

In essence, "The whole nation was to act as mediators of God's grace to the nations of the earth, even as Abraham had been promised that through him and his seed all the nations of the earth would be blessed."[3]

When Moses descended the mountain and delivered this message to the elders, "all the people answered together and said, 'All that the Lord has spoken we will do!'" (vv. 7–8a). With the people's commitment given, Moses again climbed the mountain and reported the people's response to the Lord (v. 8b). The Lord then told Moses,

> "Behold, I will come to you in a thick cloud, so that
> the people may hear when I speak with you and may
> also believe in you forever." (v. 9a)

God wanted the Israelites to listen to His laws and trust His chosen leader, Moses. He wanted them to have a sensitivity to hear and heed both of them. By coming just to Moses in a thick cloud and speaking directly with him, God was showing the people that "Moses was the recipient and mediator of the revelation of God."[4] Moses was the one to stand in the gap between the holiness of God and the sinfulness of the people.

Preparing for God's Presence

In this role, Moses was to bring God's next command to the Hebrews, which required them to undergo a time of consecration—both of body and of heart.

> "Go to the people and consecrate them today and
> tomorrow, and let them wash their garments; and
> let them be ready for the third day, for on the third
> day the Lord will come down on Mount Sinai in
> the sight of all the people." (vv. 10–11)

The Israelites needed clean clothes as well as unsoiled souls for their meeting with God. Their outer cleanliness would reflect their inner purity. With their hearts and minds aligned to God, only one more preparation needed to be made.

3. Kaiser, "Exodus," p. 416.

4. C. F. Keil and F. Delitzsch, *The Pentateuch,* in *The Biblical Commentary on the Old Testament,* trans. James Martin (Grand Rapids, Mich.: William B. Eerdmans Publishing Co, n.d.), vol. 2, p. 101.

"You shall set bounds for the people all around, saying, 'Beware that you do not go up on the mountain or touch the border of it; whoever touches the mountain shall surely be put to death. No hand shall touch him, but he shall surely be stoned or shot through; whether beast or man, he shall not live.' When the ram's horn sounds a long blast, they shall come up to the mountain." (vv. 12–13)

The Israelites needed to respect the Lord so deeply and profoundly that they would not even touch the place that marked His presence. For because of His presence, that place had become holy, and God's holiness would consume the people because of their sins. As the writer of Hebrews said, "Our God is a consuming fire" (Heb. 12:29), and out of protection for His people, He made sure that Moses and the people realized how inviolate these boundaries must be.

Encountering the Almighty

Once the Israelites finished fulfilling all the requirements God had given them, they would awake on the third day to a storm they would never forget.

*T*wilight descended on the Israelites as they camped at the foot of Mount Sinai. The setting sun cast a luminescent glow on the wisps of cloud streaking the sky. As minutes passed, the clouds turned from bright pink to deep burgundy.

In the last rays of light, the Hebrews made their final preparations for their meeting with God. Just as He had commanded, they washed their tunics and cloaks, stayed clear of the foot of the mountain, and abstained from sexual relations to avoid ceremonial defilement.

As sunrise broke over the horizon, claps of thunder began to wake the people and the ground started to shake. Emanating from the thick cloud that descended on the mountain were lightning bolts that violently struck the mountainside and came closer and closer to the camp. The thunder clapped louder and the earth quaked harder, as if trying to shake off the sting of the lightning.

Then huge billows of gray smoke began to tumble down the slope of the mountain, and a trumpet roared from the peak. It sounded like the shofar—a long, deep, bellowing cry. The trumpet blared so loudly that the people covered their ears and yelled out for Moses.

Even Moses was "full of fear and trembling" at the cosmic upheaval caused by God's approach (Heb. 12:21). With all the clouds and lightning and quaking, it must have looked like a volcanic eruption without the lava. Yet he gathered his courage and spoke to the Lord, and "God answered him with thunder" (Exod. 19:19). Then

> the Lord came down on Mount Sinai, to the top of the mountain; and the Lord called Moses to the top of the mountain, and Moses went up. Then the Lord spoke to Moses, "Go down, warn the people, so that they do not break through to the Lord to gaze, and many of them perish. Also let the priests who come near to the Lord consecrate themselves, or else the Lord will break out against them." Moses said to the Lord, "The people cannot come up to Mount Sinai, for You warned us, saying, 'Set bounds about the mountain and consecrate it.'" Then the Lord said to him, "Go down and come up again, you and Aaron with you; but do not let the priests and the

people break through to come up to the Lord, or He will break forth upon them." So Moses went down to the people and told them. (vv. 20–25)

"The Lord came down"—what a beautiful picture of the Lord's condescending grace, seen in its ultimate form in God coming down to become a man in Jesus Christ. But what are we to make of Moses' trips up and down the mountain? They show us two important truths.

First, they reinforce Moses', as well as Aaron's, role as mediator between the people and God. Not even the priests (who were perhaps the elders, since the Aaronic priesthood hadn't been established yet) could presume to come to God on their own initiative apart from God's call. These verses, observes commentator John Durham, are primarily here "to avoid any impression that Israel might approach Yahweh without a priestly/prophetic intermediary."[5] In this role, Moses and Aaron prefigure Christ, our ultimate Mediator.

But there's another reason, as scholars Keil and Delitzsch point out.

> This repeated enforcement of the command not to touch the mountain, and the special extension of it even to the priests, were intended to awaken in the people a consciousness of their own unholiness quite as much as of the unapproachable holiness of Jehovah.[6]

As the people stood trembling before the terrifying manifestation of God's unapproachable presence, they were taught that God wanted to establish a healthy fear of the Almighty to deter sin. Moses himself reinforced this truth after receiving God's first ten commandments:

> "Do not be afraid; for God has come in order to test you, and in order that the fear of Him may remain with you, so that you may not sin." (20:20)

With the Ten Commandments, God began revealing to Moses something He had never revealed before. As we'll see in more detail in our next chapter, Moses was about to receive God's first written instructions for the people to obey. They will include His sacred Law, which will not only teach the people how to live as a "kingdom of priests" and a "holy nation" but will also reveal the righteous

---

5. Durham, *Exodus*, p. 272.

6. Keil and Delitzsch, *The Pentateuch*, p. 103.

and merciful nature of the Lord. And they will receive the design of the tabernacle, where the people would know God's nearness and learn how to worship Him appropriately.

Applying the Truth for Today

In light of the majesty and awe of God we've seen in Exodus 19, perhaps it is time to examine how we view and approach God. Too many of us have a shallow concept of Him, and as a consequence, we have an anemic walk with God.

The Lord is not a kindly old grandpa or a neighborly buddy. Nor is He a rigid disciplinarian or a frigid legalist. He's the Creator, who spun the galaxies in their courses, and the Sustainer, who gives and takes life according to His infinite wisdom. He's also the Reconciler, who lowered Himself to be born in a stable and laid in a feeding trough for our sake, we who didn't deserve redeeming.

He deserves our utmost reverence and obedience. When we grasp this truth in our minds and embrace it with all our hearts, then we are ready to meet God.

We may never experience an earthly encounter with the Lord the way the Hebrews did, and we were probably never meant to. But we can be better prepared to meet with Him in the spiritual sense. Let's explore this in our Living Insights.

 Living Insights

Joshua fell on the ground in worship when he met with God (Josh. 5:14). Isaiah trembled in fear when he encountered the Holy Lord (Isa. 6:1–5). How about you? What happens when you meet with God in His Word? For many of us, our quiet times lack that sense of reverence and awe. We even find ourselves staring at a blank wall or even nodding off from time to time.

What's at the root of our blasé attitudes? Quite probably, a lack of preparation, both for our minds and our hearts. So let's establish some basic principles drawn from Exodus 19 that can help us in this essential area.

1. *To meet regularly with God, we need a place.* It may be a room in our home, a spot in our office, or a place outdoors. But whatever the location, it should be accessible, private, quiet, and conducive to study and prayer. Where's your place?

Is it comfortable, well-lit, quiet—conducive to studying, praying, and listening?

_____

_____

2. *To approach God, we need time.* Don't rush into God's presence; take time. Even before you sit down, think about who God is. Take time to read one of the psalms that extol His glory and majesty, His mercy and grace. Take time to readjust your attitude— if your mind is idle and your spirit flippant, address that. Approach God's throne with the willingness to obey, the sensitivity to hear, the desire to be cleansed . . . and with the respect He deserves.

How much time each day do you spend with the Lord?

_____

_____

Have you ever thought of spending thirty minutes a day with your Creator and Redeemer? What could you shift in your schedule to make more time for Him?

_____

_____

_____

_____

What can you do to nurture humility and respect for God, as well as an active mind and a willing heart?

_____

_____

_____

_____

3. To hear from God, we need His Word. The only written revelation we have from God is the Bible. Through His Word He speaks, teaches, exhorts, and encourages us. Hit-and-miss reading of Scripture, however, rarely reaps a rich reward. God's thoughts are more organized and integrated than that, so we need to follow His orderly lead. What is your personal method of Bible study? Take a moment to outline the steps you take.

_____

_____

_____

_____

_____

Is it more hit-and-miss than systematic? Are you gaining a greater understanding of God's Word within its context? If you need some help learning how to study the Bible and take in its truths, the following resources can help: John F. Balchin, David H. Fiel, and Tremper Longman III, eds., *The Complete Bible Study Tool Kit* (Downers Grove, Ill.: InterVarsity Press, 1991); and Jack Kuhatschek, *Taking the Guesswork Out of Applying the Bible* (Downers Grove, Ill.: InterVarsity Press, 1990).

4. To remember what God says, we need a journal. This should be a record of your spiritual walk with God, not a diary of your daily activities. You might want to write out some of your prayers, record some of the lessons you've learned from Scripture, or express concerns about your circumstances or relationships.

If you currently keep a journal, how has it helped your view of God?

_____

_____

_____

If you don't use a journal, write out the day this week you plan to start.

_____

Chapter 16

GRACE ETCHED IN STONE

Exodus 20:1–17

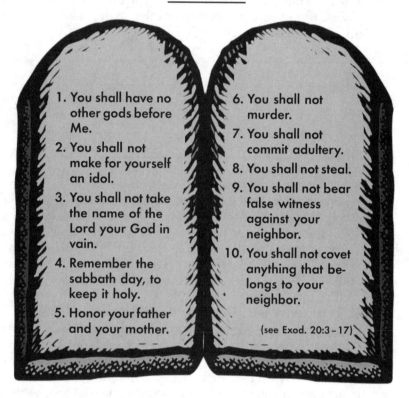

1. You shall have no other gods before Me.
2. You shall not make for yourself an idol.
3. You shall not take the name of the Lord your God in vain.
4. Remember the sabbath day, to keep it holy.
5. Honor your father and your mother.
6. You shall not murder.
7. You shall not commit adultery.
8. You shall not steal.
9. You shall not bear false witness against your neighbor.
10. You shall not covet anything that belongs to your neighbor.

(see Exod. 20:3–17)

The Ten Commandments. That's why Moses was on Mount Sinai with the Lord. Not for himself, but for his people. As mediator between the Hebrews and the Lord, Moses delivered God's standards for holy living to the community of Israel. With these laws before them, they would always have a clear understanding of what God expected of them—lives that reflected His holy nature. As *The Nelson Study Bible* explains, Moses' giving of the Law marked a new stage in Israel's relationship with the Lord.

This message was not a part of the original series but is compatible with it.

Encamped before Mount Sinai, the Israelites encountered their God, who had recently delivered them from Egyptian slavery (Gen. 12:1–13; Ex. 12; 13). At this mountain for the first time, God made a covenant with the entire nation of Israel (chs. 19–24), usually referred to as the Mosaic covenant. He formalized His relationship with the Israelites with a *suzerain-vassal* (ruler-subject) treaty. That is, God came to the Israelites as the Great King and presented to them a binding treaty in which He would make certain promises to them and they would have certain obligations as His servants.[1]

In light of this new development, the Hebrews needed to know how to conduct themselves under the covenant.

As part of this treaty, God graciously instructed the Israelites on how they should live (ch. 20). As a people who had a relationship with the living God, the Israelites had to act a certain way—God's way. The Law was benevolent instruction from God Himself. It was God's direction, like an outstretched hand pointing out the way one should take on the road of life. The Israelites were in a most enviable position. God had demonstrated His love for them by saving them. He had shown His faithfulness to His promises to their parents, Abraham and Sarah. He had formalized His relationship with them in a treaty and promised to make them His special people. Finally He gave them instruction for how to live.[2]

What a momentous occasion for the Hebrews! And what a pivotal point in their history. Their entire past, from the calling of Abraham to their deliverance from Egypt, had led up to this—the occasion on which God would deliver to them the centerpiece of His Law: the Ten Commandments.

---

1. "The Mosaic Covenant," *The Nelson Study Bible*, ed. Earl D. Radmacher (Nashville, Tenn.: Thomas Nelson Publishers, 1997), p. 134.

2. "The Mosaic Covenant," *The Nelson Study Bible*, p. 134.

Six Insights into the Ten Commandments

As we think about God's Law, we need to lay a groundwork of fundamental truths that will help us understand the nature of these ten commands.

1. *They originated from God.* These laws are not the work of human minds, which are all too often prone to prejudice, expedience, compromise, and self-interest. Instead, they came from God Himself, so we can be sure that they are fair, righteous, perfect, and holy.

2. *They express His will for His people.* They are objective and straightforward, removing all guesswork about what God desires from us.

3. *They are commands, not suggestions.* They are to be obeyed, not considered or disputed. The authority of God undergirds them.

4. *They are clear, simple, and exact.* Although many people have tried to find loopholes in these laws, their precision and clarity leave little room for creative interpretation or manipulation.

5. *There are only ten of them.* These Ten Commandments communicate the essence of God's Law in the rest of Exodus, Leviticus, Numbers, and Deuteronomy. They tell us how to love and honor God and our neighbor. By crystallizing His instructions into these ten commands, God shows that He is the master of concise truth. The human race, with its thousands of laws, cannot duplicate the relevance, comprehensiveness, and brevity of the Decalogue.

6. *They establish a healthy fear of God.* By their very nature, the Ten Commandments define transgression and imply judgment for disobedience. Who can give a command but the One who can execute punishment?

The Purpose of the Law

A crucial part of understanding the nature of the Law is knowing its purpose. What are some of the things God's Law does?

It Reveals God's Expectations

The Law makes God's desires plain and easy to grasp. We never have to wallow in doubt over whether an action or thought is right or wrong. God has removed all the guesswork in regard to our obedience. And His Ten Commandments don't change over time.

They stand in stone—absolute, immutable, permanent—marking the path of righteous living for all generations.

It Provides Us with Social and Personal Directives

We live in a fallen world where morality is defined by what feels right or what the majority decides is practical. God's Law, however, removes all ambiguity about what is best by giving us a single, clear set of ethics for society and our personal lives.

It Offers a Model for Teaching and Training Our Children

In order to lead healthy, godly lives, our children need to know and respect where right stops and wrong starts. Moses describes God's educational program for every home in Deuteronomy 6.

> "Hear, O Israel! The Lord is our God, the Lord is one! You shall love the Lord your God with all your heart and with all your soul and with all your might. These words, which I am commanding you today, shall be on your heart. You shall teach them diligently to your sons and shall talk of them when you sit in your house and when you walk by the way and when you lie down and when you rise up." (Deut. 6:4–7)

God wants parents to teach His standards to their children every day, in every way. Later in the same chapter, Moses gives some additional advice for teaching children God's ways.

> "When your son asks you in time to come, saying, 'What do the testimonies and the statutes and the judgments mean which the Lord our God commanded you?' then you shall say to your son, 'We were slaves to Pharaoh in Egypt, and the Lord brought us from Egypt with a mighty hand. Moreover, the Lord showed great and distressing signs and wonders before our eyes against Egypt, Pharaoh and all his household; He brought us out from there in order to bring us in, to give us the land which He had sworn to our fathers.' So the Lord commanded us to observe all these statutes, to fear the Lord our God *for our good always* and for survival, as it is today." (vv. 20–24, emphasis added)

God wants all His people, whether they be ancient Hebrews or Christians living today, to tell their children how He has protected and provided for them—and how we are to "walk in a manner worthy of the God who calls [us] into His own kingdom and glory" (1 Thess. 2:12).

It Reveals Our Sinfulness and Convinces Us of Our Need for a Savior

This principle reveals the central purpose for the Law. God designed it to convince people of their sinful state and of their need for a Savior. After all, who would feel the need for a Savior unless they became convinced they were destined for punishment? And who would realize they were destined for punishment unless they were persuaded they were sinners? The Law is the persuader. Everyone falls short. All are guilty. And everyone needs a Savior. No section of Scripture makes this truth more clear than the story of the golden calf.

Shortly after the Israelites had received the Ten Commandments from Moses and devoutly promised, "All the words which the Lord has spoken we will do!" (Exod. 24:3b), they transgressed the first and second commandments. These people, who had recently seen the glory of God as it thundered atop Mount Sinai, only forty days later made sacrifices to a gold-plated image of a calf. What a window into mankind's depravity! And the consequence for that depravity is judgment.

Just like the Israelites, all people are destined for punishment, because all people have a fallen nature. The Law simply identifies the ways in which we sin. By identifying our sin, however, the Law does more than condemn us—it points us to Christ. Because of this fact, we should view the Law as a benevolent teacher instead of a cold-hearted disciplinarian. The apostle Paul brought this perspective to light in his letter to the Galatians.

> Therefore the Law has become our tutor to lead us to Christ, so that we may be justified by faith. (Gal. 3:24)

Let the Law point you to Christ. Let's explore the personal applications of this in the Living Insights section.

Living Insights

John Stott accurately and beautifully describes the significance of the Law.

> Not until the law has bruised and smitten us will we admit our need for the gospel to bind up our wounds. Not until the law has arrested and imprisoned us will we pine for Christ to set us free. Not until the law has condemned and killed us will we call upon Christ for justification and life. Not until the Law has driven us to despair of ourselves will we ever believe in Jesus.[3]

Where do you stand in regard to the Law? Are you condemned by it or freed from it? If you have not yet trusted in Jesus Christ for the forgiveness of your sins, a guilty verdict stands against you. If you were to die this moment, you would spend eternity in hell.

However, you can receive a pardon from God by placing your faith in His Son. The Bible says, "He who conceals his transgressions will not prosper, But he who confesses and forsakes them will find compassion" (Prov. 28:13). God wants to extend His compassion to you. He wants to forgive you. But you must acknowledge your sin and trust in Christ.

Paul clearly described what every person must do to be saved:

> If you confess with your mouth the Lord Jesus and believe in your heart that God has raised Him from the dead, you will be saved. For with the heart one believes unto righteousness, and with the mouth confession is made unto salvation. (Rom. 10:9–10 NKJV)

If you have put your faith in Christ, you need to know several things. First, you never need to question your salvation. Christ promised that He would respond to anyone who called upon Him (Acts 2:21). Second, your salvation does not depend on your emotions. Salvation is a fact, not a feeling. If you have trusted in Christ, you are saved. Finally, you need to grow in your newfound faith. Read the Bible, pray, and find a Bible-teaching church. And, if you

---

3. John R. W. Stott, *The Message of Galatians: Only One Way* (Downers Grove, Ill.: Inter-Varsity Press, 1968), p. 93.

have any questions about salvation, spiritual growth, or finding a good church, please contact Insight for Living (see the ordering information for our address, phone numbers, and web site).

Digging Deeper

Chapters 25–40 of the book of Exodus is dedicated to the construction and operation of the tabernacle, the place God designated for sacrifice and worship during the Israelites' nomadic days. The largest section of the book, these sixteen chapters provide God's detailed instructions about the tabernacle—its dimensions, materials, maintenance, and purity.

Why such an emphasis on building a tent in the desert? What do rams' skins, wooden poles, and sacrifices have to do with spiritual life? Pastor and author James Montgomery Boice explains the ultimate lesson of the tabernacle.

> We have a dramatization of the holiness of God in the laws given for the building of the Jewish tabernacle. On one level, the tabernacle was constructed to teach the immanence of God, the truth that God is always present with his people. But on the other hand, it also taught that God is separated from his people because of his holiness and their sin, and can therefore be approached only in the way he determines. . . . The point of the tabernacle was that a sinful man or woman could not simply "barge in" upon the Holy One. God was understood to have dwelt symbolically within the innermost chamber of the tabernacle, known as the "Holy of Holies." . . . Only one person could ever go in; that was the high priest of Israel; and even he could go in only once a year and that only after having first made sacrifices for himself and the people in the outer courtyard.[4]

The writer of Hebrews revealed later in the New Testament that the tabernacle worship symbolized Christ:

> But when Christ appeared as a high priest of the

4. James Montgomery Boice, *Foundations of the Christian Faith*, rev. ed. (Downers Grove, Ill.: InterVarsity Press, 1986), pp. 128–29.

good things to come, He entered through the greater and more perfect tabernacle, not made with hands, that is to say, not of this creation; and not through the blood of goats and calves, but through His own blood, He entered the holy place once for all, having obtained eternal redemption. For if the blood of goats and bulls and the ashes of a heifer sprinkling those who have been defiled, sanctify for the cleansing of the flesh, how much more will the blood of Christ, who through the eternal Spirit offered Himself without blemish to God, cleanse your conscience from dead works to serve the living God? (Heb. 9:11–14; see also 8:1–6)

By sacrificing His own Son, who bore our sins on His body when He hung on the cross, God through Jesus has given access to the Holy One. Jesus is our High Priest, clean and pure. Look closely at the closing chapters of Exodus, and you'll see more than blueprints for a tent. You'll see the nail prints of a Savior.[5]

5. This Digging Deeper is adapted from God's Masterwork: Genesis through Second Chronicles, vol. 1, coauthored by Gary Matlack, from the Bible-teaching ministry of Charles R. Swindoll (Anaheim, Calif.: Insight for Living, 1996), pp. 24–25.

Chapter 17

THE PLACE OF THE LAW

Selected Scriptures

Just what is a Christian to make of the Law?

In the previous chapter, we identified several purposes for the Law. One of those was that the Law points us to Christ. God's perfect Law, which sinners are unable to keep, shows us our need for a Savior. If we miss that truth and reduce the Law to a set of shallow moral codes that we think we can keep, we distort the Law, impugn grace, and end up legalists.

But what about after we come to faith in Christ? What purpose does the Law serve for believers? We can, in the interest of avoiding legalism, throw out the Law altogether. But then we drift toward the other end of the spectrum, toward libertinism.

A biblical view of the Law neither overemphasizes nor ignores it. Rather, a balanced perspective properly places the Law in the context of Christian liberty. We'll present that perspective in a moment, but first we need to further examine some popular, un-balanced views of the Law.

Unhealthy Views of the Law

Antinomianism

Antinomianism means "against the Law." This word describes people who have little or no respect for God's Law. They may be unbelievers who have adopted a humanistic way of thinking that throws off moral restrictions. To them, the very idea of an objective set of religious codes is an outdated concept. From their perspective, the Law is no more than a relic of earlier, narrow-minded times.

Antinomians, though, may also include some believers—people in the church who don't see the Law as relevant for Christians. While this group acknowledges that the Law is noble and good, they say it no longer has relevance for those who have found spiritual freedom through faith in Christ. Because Christians have been

---

This message was not part of the original series but is compatible with it.

freed from the curse of the Law, they argue, believers have no further use for the Law. Christians, then, might as well tear the Ten Commandments out of their Bibles.

Antinomianism has been around for centuries. Martin Luther, for example, faced off with one of his students, Johann Agricola over this very issue. Agricola denied that the Law had any purpose in the life of the believer or that it even prepared the sinner for grace. Luther responded with a treatise entitled *Against the Antinomians*. Agricola recanted, but antinomianism still remains alive and well.

Believers who embrace antinomianism often show contempt for those who hold a deep respect for the Law, classifying them as legalists or supporters of salvation-by-works.

This antinomian attitude grossly misrepresents the relationship between the Law and salvation. The Law, as we will see later, does have a place in the life of a believer.

Legalism

On the opposite end of the spectrum from the antinomians are the legalists. Rather than ignoring the Law, they believe that we can actually keep the Law and thus gain a righteous standing before God. Salvation, then, comes through keeping the Law, not through faith in Christ. People in this theological camp disagree about the number and kinds of laws they believe must be obeyed, but they all agree that some kind of obedience to God's Law is necessary for eternal life. Like antinomianism, legalism has been around for centuries. We even see it in the Scriptures.

The Pharisees, for example, were noted for their self-righteous adherence to the Law. Their "law," though, was their own system of rigid rule-keeping, not the true Law of God, which demanded both inward and outward conformity.

The apostle Paul had to confront legalism in his dealings with the church in Galatia, a church he had founded. The Galatians had fallen under the spell of the Judaizers, who taught that faith in Christ alone was insufficient for salvation. They taught that people must also obey the ceremonial mandates of the Law, particularly the Jewish rite of circumcision. The book of Galatians is Paul's denunciation of legalism and his defense of the doctrine of justification by faith alone. In this letter, he makes a clear distinction between works and salvation.

We are Jews by nature and not sinners from among

the Gentiles; nevertheless knowing that a man is not justified by the works of the Law but through faith in Christ Jesus, even we have believed in Christ Jesus, so that we may be justified by faith in Christ and not by the works of the Law; since by the works of the Law no flesh will be justified. (Gal. 2:15–16)

Obedience to the Law can never save. Circumcision couldn't do it for the Judaizers. And we can't keep the Law today. Only one Person kept the Law perfectly—Jesus Christ. And when we believe in Him, His perfect righteousness is transferred to our account. God sees us, then, clothed in the righteousness of His own dear Son . . . and accepts us.

Faith in the Lord Jesus Christ saves us. Period. Not keeping the Law. Not abstaining from movies, secular music, tobacco, or alcohol. Christ alone is our salvation.

Limitations of the Law

The Law actually has limitations as to what it can accomplish. Not because it's weak, but because we are.

It Cannot Set Us Free

Everyone without Christ is shackled by sin. We are imprisoned, and God's sentence of judgment hangs over our heads. The Law makes us aware of our dilemma; it shows us our sin. But it cannot free us from those circumstances.

But before faith came, we were kept in custody under the law, being shut up to the faith which was later to be revealed. (Gal. 3:23)

The Law, then, acts as a jail warden—a constant reminder of our powerlessness to escape our sinful condition and our inability to comply with God's standards. And only faith in Jesus Christ can set us free.

For the law of the Spirit of life in Christ Jesus has set you free from the law of sin and of death. For what the Law could not do, weak as it was through the flesh, God did: sending His own Son in the likeness of sinful flesh and as an offering for sin, He condemned sin in the flesh. (Rom. 8:2–3)

It Cannot Justify Us before God

As imprisoned sinners with a guilty plea on our record and a death sentence looming, we need a court ruling that will clear our names and set us free. In other words, we need to be justified. Robert Lightner notes, "Justification is the work of God by which He declares the believing sinner righteous before Him."[1] Justification is a legal ruling, and the Law has no power to make such an acquittal; the Law only condemns.

> Now that no one is justified by the Law before God
> is evident; for, "The righteous man shall live by faith."
> However, the Law is not of faith. (Gal. 3:11–12a)

No one is justified by the Law. It cannot remove our guilt; it only intensifies it. Only faith in Jesus Christ can set us free and make us righteous in God's eyes. What *does* the Law do, then?

Uses of the Law

Theologians talk about the "threefold use of the Law." Together, these uses give us a full picture of why God gave us His Law and how the Law relates to grace.

The Law Serves as a Mirror, Showing Us Our Sin

When we hold God's Law up before us, we see who God is—perfectly righteous—and who we are—sinful people, unable to work our way to God. We are condemned by our deeds, standing in the path of God's judgment. Paul tells us that

> by the works of the Law no flesh will be justified in
> His sight; for through the Law comes knowledge of
> sin. (Rom. 3:20; see also Rom. 7:7–12)

The Law shows us "our need of pardon and our danger of damnation"[2] so that we may run in repentance and faith to Christ (see Gal. 3:19–24). This use of the Law leads unbelievers to faith in Christ, and it leads believers to repentance and restored fellowship when they transgress God's Law.

---

1. Robert P. Lightner, *Sin, the Savior, and Salvation: The Theology of Everlasting Life* (Nashville, Tenn.: Thomas Nelson Publishers, 1991), p. 212.

2. *New Geneva Study Bible* (Nashville, Tenn.: Thomas Nelson Publishers, 1995), p. 259.

The Law Serves as a Policeman, Enforcing Order

Theologians also speak of the "civil use" of the Law.

> Though the law cannot change the heart, it can to
> some extent inhibit lawlessness by its threats of judg-
> ment, especially when backed by a civil code that
> administers punishment for proven offenses (Deut.
> 13:6–11; 19:16–21; Rom. 13:3, 4).[3]

This use of the Law is primarily for unbelievers, since, as the
third use reveals, Christians should strive to abide by God's Law
out of gratitude and love for Him, not out fear of judgment.

The Law Serves as a Guide, Leading Us into Good Works

This third function of the Law

> guide[s] the regenerate into the good works that God
> has planned for them (Eph. 2:10). The law tells
> God's children what will please their heavenly Fa-
> ther. It could be called their family code. Christ was
> speaking of this third use of the law when He said
> that those who become His disciples must be taught
> to do all that He had commanded (Matt. 28:20),
> and that obedience to His commands will prove the
> reality of one's love for Him (John 14:15). The
> Christian is free from the law as a system of salvation
> (Rom. 6:14; 7:4, 6; 1 Cor. 9:20; Gal. 2:15–19; 3:25),
> but is "under law toward Christ" as a rule of life
> (1 Cor. 9:21; Gal. 6:2).[4]

The Law, then, does apply to believers. It tells us how to live
holy lives, how to love God and our neighbor, how to keep God
at the forefront of our lives. King David expressed his desire to love
God by keeping His commands:

> I will meditate on Your precepts
> And regard Your ways.
> I shall delight in Your statutes;
> I shall not forget Your word. (Ps. 119:15–16)

---

3. *New Geneva Study Bible,* p. 259.

4. *New Geneva Study Bible,* p. 259.

So, as Christians, we should strive in the power of the Holy Spirit to live in a way that pleases God—out of gratitude and love for Him, not out of the fear of judgment or the belief that we can work our way to heaven in our own power. And when we fail to keep God's Law, we know our shortcomings don't condemn us. For we are clothed in the righteousness of Christ, who kept the Law perfectly on our behalf.

Our Response to the Law

Given the nature of the Law, then, how should we live?

Embrace Grace, but Don't Abuse It

We never want to give a foothold to either legalism or antinomianism. Legalism renounces grace; antinomianism abuses it. The key to properly expressing Christian liberty is simply seeking to please the Lord in everything we do.

Let Your Godly Attitudes Become Godly Actions

How we love God shows up in how we live for God. Godly attitudes are designed to produce godly actions. An attitude that fails to produce a corresponding action is like seed that fails to produce a crop. Peter, in his second letter, touched on the importance of this relationship between attitudes and actions.

> For this very reason, make every effort to add to your faith goodness; and to goodness, knowledge; and to knowledge, self-control; and to self-control, perseverance; and to perseverance, godliness; and to godliness, brotherly kindness; and to brotherly kindness, love. For if you possess these qualities in increasing measure, they will keep you from being ineffective and unproductive in your knowledge of the Lord Jesus Christ. (2 Peter 1:5–9)

Our heart, head, and hands should all be involved in loving and walking with God.

While Pursuing Righteousness, Avoid Sin

God's Law is both positive and negative. It tells us what to pursue and what to avoid. When we embrace a sinful lifestyle, we pollute our lives and dilute our witness. So we should avoid those things that can entrap us and bog us down in sin. This truth is powerfully revealed in the story of the little boy who played in the rain while wearing white gloves. His gloves became muddy, but the mud never became glovey.

The same holds true for Christians who play in sin. The sin stains the believer, but the believer never cleanses the sin. With this thought in mind, we should have only one response to sin—shun it. We should run from it as fast as we can. But when we do sin, praise God that we are kept secure in our salvation by One who never sinned. One who kept the Law without fail. One who died for us that we might live.

 Living Insights

Based on what we learned about the various views of the Law in this lesson, describe where your perspective of the Law would fall by circling a number on the scale below. Remember, an antinomian sees no use for the Law at all, and a Judaizer would believe that obedience to the Law is necessary for salvation.

5   4   3   2   1   0   1   2   3   4   5

Antinomian   *Balanced*   *Judaizer*

No matter where you are on the spectrum, hopefully this lesson has helped you see the need to have a balanced view of the Law. Take a minute to reflect on how you can better utilize the Law in your Christian walk.

What specific actions can you take to help the Law remind you of God's holy standards (memorizing it, meditating on it, etc.)?

_____

_____

_____

_____

_____

_____

What measures can you take to walk in obedience?

_____

_____

_____

_____

_____

Chapter 18

GRUMBLINGS AGAINST A GODLY LEADER
Numbers 10–14

With the sin of the golden calf, the Israelites went from being called a "holy nation" to God declaring them a "stiff-necked people" (Exod. 33:3 NIV). They were now alienated from the Lord— He even threatened to withdraw His presence as they proceeded to the Promised Land (v. 3b). Fortunately for Israel, Moses, their mediator, continued to find favor in Yahweh's sight.

God "used to speak to Moses face to face, just as a man speaks to his friend" (v. 11). So Moses interceded for the people, and God relented, promising to accompany the Israelites and renewing His covenant with them (vv. 12–17; 34:1–28). Subsequently, the Lord revealed His glory to Moses (33:18–23), whose face became radiant after he had been in the holy presence of God (34:29–35).

The remainder of Exodus records how Moses and the restored people built the tabernacle, fashioned its furnishings, and made the priestly garments according to God's directions. The place to meet with God was now constructed, His glory filling it. Now Moses needed to teach the people the way to approach their holy Lord. And this is what he did in his next book, Leviticus.

One writer notes, "Leviticus details how the Israelites were to become a holy nation—how they were to revere God and approach His presence, how they were to treat one another, and how they were to reflect God in every area of life."[1] Here the sacrificial system was instituted, as were the rules for the priests, ritual purity, and the Day of Atonement. God's holy and compassionate ethical standards were made clear here, and so were the blessings for upholding the covenant with obedience and the curses for breaking it with disobedience.

With these laws given, the people were finally prepared to move from Mount Sinai to be God's testimony in the Promised Land.

---

1. From the study guide *God's Masterwork: Genesis through Second Chronicles*, vol. 1, coauthored by Gary Matlack, from the Bible-teaching ministry of Charles R. Swindoll (Anaheim, Calif.: Insight for Living, 1996), p. 29.

This is the story of Moses' fourth book, Numbers. In the opening chapters, Moses detailed the mustering of all men over twenty for war, arranged the tribes around God's tabernacle, and established the tribes' marching order. He communicated God's further laws to ensure the people's purity, instructed Aaron in blessing the nation in Yahweh's name, and guided the Israelites in celebrating the first Passover since their deliverance from Egypt.

Then the pillar of cloud lifted from above the tabernacle, the silver trumpets sounded, and it was time to begin their journey!

On the twentieth day of the second month of their second year since the Exodus, the Hebrews gathered to leave Sinai. The tribe of Judah set out first, following their brightly colored standard with the image of a lion emblazoned on the front. Next went the host of Issachar and then the tribe of Zebulun, both marching under their banners.

Following these three tribes, the Levites bore the tabernacle materials. Behind them marched the tribes of Reuben, Simeon, and Gad. In the center of the train, the priests upheld on long staves the ark of the covenant. The three tribes of Ephraim, Manasseh, and Benjamin followed the ark; and providing the rear guard were Dan, Asher, and Naphtali.

As Moses looked upon this ocean of colors, he could see the succession of banners—and his heart pounded at the nearness of God's promise being fulfilled. During these first three days of travel, the ark moved to the front of the procession as a reminder of God's leading them. And Moses, with a burst of joy and confidence, gave this war cry:

"Rise up, O Lord!
And let Your enemies be scattered,
And let those who hate You flee before You."

From Exuberance to Exasperation

After nearly a year of God's faithful provision and guidance, as well as instruction in the character and worship of God, the Israelites must have been thrilled to follow the Lord's faithful leading to the Promised Land, right? They must have shared Moses' exuberant faith, his loving trust and gratitude toward God, and been a delight to their dedicated leader, surely!

Wrong.

They grumbled. They groused. They whined. They wailed. They were a sharp pebble in Moses' sandal. They gripped large stones and aimed them at his head.

The people's lack of faith would cost them—and Moses, their faithful leader—more dearly than they could ever have imagined.

The People Complain

After only the first three days of travel, Moses realized that many of the people didn't share his delight in what the Lord was doing for them.

> Now the people became like those who complain of adversity in the hearing of the Lord; and when the Lord heard it, His anger was kindled, and the fire of the Lord burned among them and consumed some of the outskirts of the camp. (Num. 11:1)

Surrounded by flames, the terrified Israelites "cried out to Moses" to intercede for them. Moses immediately "prayed to the Lord and the fire died out" (v. 2). This incident made such an impact on them that they even named that place Taberah, "Burning." But, amazingly, it didn't make enough of an impact to stop the complaining.

The "rabble who were among them" dared to whine and moan about how much better they had had it in Egypt, and their complaining soon spread to the rest of Israel.

> [The rabble] had greedy desires; and also the sons of Israel wept again and said, "Who will give us meat to eat? We remember the fish which we used to eat free in Egypt, the cucumbers and the melons and the leeks and the onions and the garlic, but now our appetite is gone. There is nothing at all to look at except this manna." (vv. 4–6)

"Eat *free*"—in Egypt? It only cost them the lives of their baby boys, who were thrown into the Nile by Pharaoh's servants; the lives of their husbands and brothers, who collapsed under the whips of taskmasters! Can you imagine preferring slavery and oppression to bread from heaven? Moses sure couldn't. He was "displeased" at the self-pity bawling out of every tent. So he took his distress to the Lord.

> "Why have You been so hard on Your servant? And why have I not found favor in Your sight, that you have laid the burden of all this people on me? Was it I who conceived all this people? Was it I who brought them forth, that You should say to me, 'Carry them in your bosom as a nurse carries a nursing infant, to the land which You swore to their fathers'? Where am I to get meat to give to all this people? For they weep before me, saying, 'Give us meat that we may eat!' I alone am not able to carry all this people, because it is too burdensome for me. So if you are going to deal thus with me, please kill me at once, if I have found favor in Your sight, and do not let me see my wretchedness." (vv. 11–15)

That's despair. Moses was overwhelmed and sinking fast. So, in His mercy, the Lord tended to His weary servant before addressing the ingratitude of the people. Similar to His use of Jethro's plan to give Moses relief in his judging duties, God now instructed Moses to gather seventy of Israel's leading elders at the tabernacle. Upon them the Lord would share the Spirit that had been given to Moses so that he would not have to bear the burden of the people alone (vv. 16–17).

As for the people, they would get their meat—quail for a solid month, "'until it comes out of [their] nostrils and becomes loathsome,'" God promised (vv. 18–20).

At first, Moses couldn't fathom how God could supply meat to everyone in the middle of the desert (vv. 21–22). But God countered his doubt: "Is the Lord's power limited? Now you shall see whether My word will come true for you or not" (v. 23). So Moses obediently told the people about the quail and gathered the seventy elders around the tabernacle. At the moment the Spirit was bestowed on them, they prophesied (vv. 24–25)—including two elders who hadn't come to the tabernacle but stayed in camp. Which caused a small problem.

Joshua Misunderstands

At this time in Israel's history, Moses was the only prophet among the people. But when the seventy elders prophesied, Moses lost part of his unique status. The change was a great relief to Moses. But not to his aide, Joshua. In his eyes, those two elders prophesying in the camp represented a challenge to Moses' leadership. "Moses, my lord," he protested, "restrain them" (v. 28). But Moses gently corrected him.

> "Are you jealous for my sake? Would that all the
> Lord's people were prophets, that the Lord would
> put His Spirit upon them!" (v. 29)

Moses understood that the Lord was the sovereign Head. Consequently, he looked on God's activity in the lives of others with joy rather than jealousy and was grateful for the mercy God had shown him.

God's mercy, however, was tempered with judgment when it came to the complainers. Wind-borne quail blew in from the sea, and the people spent a day and a night gathering them (vv. 31–32). But "while the meat was still between their teeth, before it was chewed," a plague struck the people who had rejected Yahweh (v. 33). They named the place of this awful memory, too—Kibroth-hattaavah, "Graves of Craving" (v. 34).

Miriam and Aaron Rebel

From the Graves of Craving, the people moved on to Hazeroth. Little time passed before Moses ran into opposition—this time from his own family. Miriam and Aaron, prejudiced against Moses' Cushite wife,[2] challenged Moses' special status with the Lord: "Has the Lord indeed spoken only through Moses? Has He not spoken through us as well?" (12:1–2). In their self-importance, they accused Moses of arrogantly appointing himself as leader, which was the furthest thing from his humble mind (v. 3).

When the Lord heard His servant slandered, He called all three of them to the tabernacle; then He singled out Miriam and Aaron.

---

2. Zipporah, Moses' first wife, had probably died, and no legal restrictions prohibited Hebrews from marrying Cushites (compare Exod. 34:11–16). But Miriam and Aaron apparently disapproved of the union—Miriam in particular might have felt that her leadership position among the women was threatened by this newcomer's status as Moses' wife.

Visions and dreams were the ways through which God spoke to other prophets, the Lord told them, but it was not that way with Moses. "With him I speak mouth to mouth, Even openly, and not in dark sayings," God said, adding, "And he beholds the form of the Lord" (vv. 7–8). "Why then," God pointedly asked them, "were you not afraid To speak against My servant, against Moses?" (v. 8b). By challenging Moses' authority, they were really challenging the Lord's choice and the work He was doing through His servant.

So He vindicated Moses and rebuked Miriam and Aaron, laying the punishment on Miriam because she had apparently incited this rebellion.[3] She became white with leprosy, and the horrified Aaron begged Moses' forgiveness. Moses swiftly interceded, but God declared that she would bear the shame of her presumption for seven days. So for one week the whole camp waited, sin delaying them again, before finally moving from Hazeroth to the desert of Paran—and the brink of the Promised Land (vv. 9–16).

From Exploration to Disqualification

The Promised Land! The covenant God had made with Abraham was about to be fulfilled. The Israelites' life as a kingdom of priests and a holy nation in a land of their own—a land of God's giving—was about to begin. It had been a long haul for Moses, but new strength came to him now. They were so close!

The People Lose Faith

When the Israelites arrived near the outskirts of the Promised Land, the Lord told Moses to send out twelve spies on a reconnaissance mission (13:1–24). They returned forty days later, with all but Caleb and Joshua quivering with a frightening report about the size and the fierceness of the land's inhabitants (vv. 25–33). Caleb tried to silence them, urging the people to "go up and take possession of [the land], for we will surely overcome it" (v. 30). However, after forty days of wondering about what the spies would find, coupled with a lifelong tendency to think the worst of the Lord, the people just weren't listening.

> Then all the congregation lifted up their voices and cried, and the people wept that night. All the

3. This deduction is based on her name initially preceding Aaron's in this account.

sons of Israel grumbled against Moses and Aaron; and the whole congregation said to them, "Would that we had died in the land of Egypt! Or would that we had died in this wilderness! Why is the Lord bringing us into this land, to fall by the sword? Our wives and our little ones will become plunder; would it not be better for us to return to Egypt?" (14:1–3)

The people even made plans to replace Moses with a new leader who would take them back to Egypt (v. 4). Fear had totally replaced their faith. In grief and in dread of the Lord's sure judgment, Moses and Aaron fell on their faces. Joshua and Caleb tore their clothes and desperately tried to turn the tide:

"The land which we passed through to spy out is an exceedingly good land. If the Lord is pleased with us, then He will bring us into this land and give it to us—a land which flows with milk and honey. Only do not rebel against the Lord; and do not fear the people of the land, for they will be our prey. Their protection has been removed from them, and the Lord is with us; do not fear them." (vv. 7b–9)

But the people had a message of their own: "Stone them!" God, however, had had enough.

The Faithless Lose the Land

The Lord said to Moses, "How long will this people spurn Me? And how long will they not believe in Me, despite all the signs which I have performed in their midst? I will smite them with pestilence and dispossess them, and I will make you into a nation greater and mightier than they." (vv. 11–12)

It is a testimony to Moses' loyalty to the people and to the glory of God's name that he pleaded with the Lord to spare the Hebrews (vv. 11–19). The Lord granted Moses' request and did not destroy them. But they would bear the consequences of slandering God's goodness.

"I have pardoned them according to your word; but indeed, as I live, all the earth will be filled with the glory of the Lord. Surely all the men who have seen My glory and My signs which I performed in Egypt and in the wilderness, yet have put Me to the test these ten times and have not listened to My voice, shall by no means see the land which I swore to their fathers, nor shall any of those who spurned Me see it. . . .

. . . "How long shall I bear with this evil congregation who are grumbling against Me? I have heard the complaints of the sons of Israel, which they are making against Me. Say to them, 'As I live' says the Lord, 'just as you have spoken in My hearing, so I will surely do to you; your corpses will fall in this wilderness, even all your numbered men, according to your complete number from twenty years old and upward, who have grumbled against Me. Surely you shall not come into the land in which I swore to settle you, except Caleb the son of Jephunneh and Joshua the son of Nun. Your children, however, whom you said would become a prey—I will bring them in, and they will know the land which you have rejected. But as for you, your corpses will fall in this wilderness. Your sons shall be shepherds for forty years in the wilderness, and they will suffer for your unfaithfulness.'" (vv. 20–23, 27–33)

One year for every day they had spied out the land would they wander in the wilderness (v. 34). The ten spies who gave the bad report and caused the people to grumble died from a plague (vv. 36–38). And the repentant Israelites, not believing it was too late and ignoring Moses' warnings, tried to invade the land and were soundly defeated (vv. 39–45).

They had been so close.

A Concluding Thought

Can you imagine the grief of Moses, Aaron, Caleb, and Joshua? Moses, especially, must have endured great waves of sorrow and pain. Constantly interceding for the people, he faced their grumbling and the discouragement it brought with humility and faith, only to have his dreams of entering the Promised Land dashed. As God had said, the children of the faithless would suffer for their parents' unfaithfulness, and so would Moses. He, too, would wander, bearing the consequences of other people's sins.

 Living Insights

Did you ever think that grumbling could have such drastic results? In our society, a cynical attitude is the norm; it's what drives so much of our humor, maintains so much of our apathy. But from these tragic chapters in Numbers, we see that God detests a grumbling spirit.

Why? Why did God take so personally the Israelites' grumbling about their circumstances and leaders? What is at the root of grumbling that makes it such a gross offense? What do you deduce from Numbers 11:20?

_____

_____

_____

What is the connection between grumbling and rejecting the Lord? Between grumbling and not believing Him? Between grumbling and treating Him with contempt?

_____

_____

_____

In their grumbling, the Israelites treated the good things from the Lord as if they were bad, which was really viewing His goodness as if it were evil. Gratitude and loving trust would have been the more appropriate responses to all that God had done and was going to do for them.

How have you, at times, acted like the ancient Israelites? Take some time now to examine what you grumble about. Are you really grumbling about God and His provision in your life?

_____

_____

Learn from the Israelites' example, won't you? God didn't include these stories in His Word to terrify us but to straighten out the paths of our wayward hearts. Ask His forgiveness, and ask Him for a heart of gratitude. Cultivate your trust in Him, because, despite what your fears may tell you, He is the most trustworthy and most good reality in your life.

Digging Deeper

Incredible as it seems, even after losing the Promised Land, that generation of grumblers was not done grumbling yet. As the Lord and Moses prepared the next generation to enter the land (Num. 15), another revolt arose against Moses and Aaron (chap. 16).

Korah, Dathan, and Abiram, along with 250 other community leaders, came as an organized group to accuse Moses and Aaron of presumptuously assuming the political and spiritual leadership of Israel (vv. 1–3). In reality, Korah and the Levites with him aspired to the priestly privilege God had bestowed on Aaron and his family, not being content with the sacred duties for which God had consecrated them (vv. 8–11). Dathan, Abiram, On, and their fellow conspirators blamed Moses for their wilderness wandering, claiming that he had ineptly led them out of a land flowing with milk and honey—Egypt(!)—and into a miserable desert (vv. 12–14).

The Lord swiftly confronted their insolence against Moses and Aaron. He defended His right to make the sovereign choices He had made by showing unmistakably who was chosen by Him and who was not (vv. 4–7, 16–19, 28–30). He caused the earth to split open and swallow alive Korah, Dathan, Abiram, and their families and possessions; then He just as suddenly closed the earth over them (vv. 31–34). And the 250 men aspiring to be priests were consumed by fire with their censers still in their hands (v. 35).

Did the rest of the community now believe that Moses and Aaron were God's chosen? Appallingly, no. The next day, they collectively grumbled against their leaders, "You have killed the

Lord's people" (v. 41). No wonder God wanted to destroy them (vv. 20, 44–45)! Moses quickly had Aaron make atonement for them, but 14,700 people were still felled by the Lord's plague of judgment (vv. 46–50).

To try to silence their grumbling once and for all, God showed His unmistakable choice of Aaron in another, less catastrophic, contest. Twelve leaders from each of the tribes were to give Moses their staffs, Aaron representing the tribe of Levi, and Moses would place them in the tabernacle (17:1–5). The person whose staff sprouted as if it were still a living branch would be the Lord's chosen—and Aaron's not only had buds but also blossomed and produced almonds (vv. 6–9)! His living staff would be a perpetual memorial to remind the people that God had chosen Aaron's line alone for the priesthood—and to quell any further presumptuous revolts (vv. 10–11).

Finally, the people confessed their sinfulness in arrogantly opposing the leaders God had chosen (vv. 12–13). And in the next two chapters, they are given the appropriate means of approaching God (chaps. 18–19).

Were they now a grumble-free people? How Moses wished they were!

Chapter 19

A MOMENT OF RAGE

Numbers 20:1–13

Moses sat alone in his tent, mourning the loss of his sister Miriam. There were so many memories of her, and right now he just wanted to lose himself in them.

He recalled the many times Miriam told him of that fateful day at the Nile—when Jochebed placed him in a basket and hid it among the reeds. How Miriam persuaded Pharaoh's daughter to have Jochebed suckle him as an infant. How that plan saved Moses' life . . . and saved Jochebed's heart from being broken.

Then Moses remembered the Red Sea. He remembered how God destroyed the Egyptians and how the people sang a song of praise right there on the beach. How Miriam took a timbrel in her hand, and with a gleam in her eyes, led the Hebrew women in a beautiful song of praise that moved Moses to tears.

Unpleasant memories came as well. Miriam never recovered from the death of Zipporah, Moses' first wife, and she could barely stand the sight of his second wife, a Cushite woman. Miriam had even challenged Moses' leadership. But Moses had found himself pleading for her life and health when the Lord struck her with leprosy for her rebellion.

Most of Moses' memories about Miriam, though, were good ones. And he relished this time to treasure them—short though it was. For the sweet calm of reminiscence was about to be shattered by a cacophony of grumbling.

Once again the camp had run short of water. And once again the Israelites would abandon their trust in God and blame Moses for their predicament. Only this time, he would show them he had had enough.

The Anger of Moses

Faith. Steadfastness. Obedience. Persistence. Moses possessed many strengths, didn't he? But even the strongest leaders have weaknesses. David committed adultery. Peter briefly drifted into legalism. And Moses? He got angry. And his anger evidenced a lapse in belief, a failure to trust God for what He promised. It's a mistake that cost him deeply . . . but one that will teach us deeply, if we'll heed the lessons from Numbers 20:1–13.

It shouldn't surprise us at all that Moses lost his temper with the Israelites. What is surprising is that he didn't lose it more often, given their forty years of constant complaining in the wilderness and their fickle faith in God. Nevertheless, Moses' actions in Numbers 20 remind us that anger—especially when it overshadows the will of God and obscures His holiness—often produces dire consequences.

Still Grumbling after All These Years

Thirty-nine years. That's how long the children of Israel had been wandering in the wilderness. Most of the older generation, including Miriam, were dead. Death in the wilderness was God's punishment on Israel for their failure to move into the Promised Land at Kadesh Barnea (see Num. 14). Now the new generation was back at Kadesh. And guess what? They were not doing much better than their parents. When hardship hit, their first response was to assign blame instead of trusting God.

There was no water for the congregation, and they assembled themselves before Moses and Aaron. The people thus contended with Moses and spoke, saying, "If only we had perished when our brothers perished before the Lord! Why then have you brought the Lord's assembly into this wilderness, for us and our beasts to die here? Why have you made us come up from Egypt, to bring us in to this wretched place? It is not a place of grain or figs or vines or pomegranates, nor is there water to drink." (20: 2–5)

Sound familiar? Their complaint has an all-too-common ring (see Exod. 16:3; 17:1–3; Num. 14:1–3). Facing the threat of a mutiny, Moses and Aaron ran to the Lord in prayer. Notice the specific instructions God gave to the two leaders.

God's Instructions

"Take the rod; and you and your brother Aaron assemble the congregation and speak to the rock before their eyes, that it may yield its water. You shall thus bring forth water for them out of the rock and let the congregation and their beasts drink." (v. 8)

God's directions were clear: "Speak to the rock." Moses was not to touch the rock or speak to the people. Notice what he did.

So Moses took the rod from before the Lord, just as He had commanded him; and Moses and Aaron gathered the assembly before the rock. And he said to them, "Listen now, you rebels; shall we bring forth water for you out of this rock?" Then Moses lifted up his hand and struck the rock twice with his rod; and water came forth abundantly, and the congregation and their beasts drank. (vv. 9–11)

Did you notice the difference between the Lord's command and what Moses actually did? Moses used the opportunity to scold the people, and he also hit the rock with his staff in anger. God still miraculously provided water, but He sternly rebuked Moses and Aaron for their disobedience.

But the Lord said to Moses and Aaron, "Because you have not believed Me, to treat Me as holy in the sight of the sons of Israel, therefore you shall not bring this assembly into the land which I have given them." Those were the waters of Meribah,[1] because the sons of Israel contended with the Lord, and He proved Himself holy among them. (vv. 12–13)

If Moses had only spoken to the rock, then the miracle would have pointed to God's power and provision. Instead, he rebuked the Hebrews and brought attention to himself. He distracted the people from the Lord. As a result, the Lord denied both him and Aaron entrance into the Promised Land.

Too Harsh a Penalty?

Doesn't this seem extreme? With all the good that Moses had done, why would God be so harsh on His faithful servant for this one infraction? Several things must be considered here.

First, Moses was a leader—the mediator of the covenant between God and the people of Israel. With such a position comes great responsibility. "From everyone who has been given much, much will be required; and to whom they entrusted much, of him they will ask all the more" (Luke 12:48). By disobeying God's command, Moses and Aaron, in a sense, usurped God's authority; they put themselves in charge. They trusted and believed in themselves more than they did in God. And the Israelites were disobedient enough; they didn't need any encouragement from leadership to stray from the Lord.

Second, God's punishment of Moses reminds us that no one, not even the great deliverer and lawgiver, is perfect. Moses was the covenant mediator for the people. He interceded for them. He was the reflection of God's power, glory, judgment and mercy. Yet he, too, was a sinner in need of God's grace. His imperfections direct us to the only perfect Mediator and Intercessor, Jesus Christ.

Finally, we must remember that, though Moses was denied entrance into the earthly Promised Land, he entered the heavenly Promised Land upon his death in Moab. He had a long and fruitful ministry, then entered the presence of the Lord. He went from grumbling to glory, from wandering to rest. In that sense, his punishment was really a blessing.

---

1. The name *Meribah* (along with the name *Massah*) was used forty years earlier for the place where God first brought water from a rock (see Exod. 17:1–7).

Living Insights

Numbers 20 reminds us that a momentary loss of self-control can yield serious consequences and adversely affect our walk with God. Have you encountered any times in your life when you've lost your cool and suffered the consequences? Think of a specific incident and write out your recollections below.

Did your act stem from unbelief in some way? Describe it.

_____

_____

_____

_____

Did your flare-up cause you to diminish your witness or God's glory? How?

_____

_____

_____

_____

What consequences did you suffer?

_____

_____

_____

Given the same circumstances, what would you do differently?

_____

_____

_____

_____

Chapter 20

FILLING THE SHOES
OF MOSES

Numbers 27:12–23

The 1936 Olympic Games, held in Berlin, will forever occupy a special place in sports history. Most people will remember the Games for the performance of Jesse Owens, an African-American runner who won four gold medals as a stunned Adolph Hitler watched. Hitler wanted to use the Games to showcase the superiority of his Aryan athletes. His plan backfired. But Jesse Owens wasn't the only reason the Nazis were upstaged.

Germany had the fastest women's 400 meter relay team in the world. Their only competition came from the United States team, anchored by Helen Stephens, the world's fastest woman.

During the semi-finals, the German team won their heat and established a new world record. The Americans, too, won their heat, running only seven-tenths of a second slower than the Germans. Going into the finals, the Germans developed a clever plan to try to overcome the incredible speed of Miss Stephens. They placed their fastest runners in the first three legs of the race, hoping the three would build up a lead that even Stephens couldn't overcome. The German plan seemed flawless. But it was only as flawless as their fourth runner.

Ilse Dorffeldt, the new German anchor, had two images emblazoned on her mind. First, the image of Helen Stephens crossing the finish line in the 100-meter dash, where she dominated and set a new world record just a few days earlier. Second, Dorffeldt could see the stern face of her führer, Adolph Hitler. He would be watching her from his balcony in the stadium. He expected perfection from his athletes — especially now, when the whole world was watching.

As the race began, the first two German sprinters accomplished their task by establishing a strong lead over the Americans. The third runner, Marie Dollinger, stretched the lead to an insurmountable eight meters. It looked as though the German team would win, and the Nazis would have their prize. All Ilse had to do was grab the baton from her teammate and sprint to the finish line.

Striding uncontested, with her eyes fixed on the open track,

Ilse reached back to take the baton . . . but she felt only air. She wheeled around and finally clutched the stick, but it slipped out of her sweat-covered hand and onto the track. No one will ever know if Helen Stephens could have overcome that eight-meter deficit. But the Americans won that day. And the Germans lost—because they failed to pass the baton.

Anyone who cares about human rights is delighted that Ilse Dorffeldt fumbled that baton and embarrassed the Nazi regime. But dropping the baton can also hinder the progress of more benevolent organizations. Christian ministries and churches, for example, run the risk of falling by the wayside if their outgoing leaders fail to pass the baton of leadership to the next generation. And no one knew that better than Moses.

The Promised Land in Sight

Tears must have welled up in Moses' eyes as he stood with the people on the banks of the Jordan River, peering into the Promised Land. The Lord's judgment still echoed in his mind.

> "Because you have not believed Me, to treat Me as holy in the sight of the sons of Israel, therefore you shall not bring this assembly into the land which I have given them." (Num. 20:12)

Piercing through Moses' disappointment, though, came the stark reality that Israel needed a suitable replacement—someone to help them conquer and settle in the land of Canaan. How could the right person be found? Who would he be? Numbers 27:12–23 tells us how Moses passed the baton of leadership for the welfare of the next generation of Hebrews. In that passage, we'll discover some timeless truths that will help us as we seek to fill positions of leadership in our churches and other organizations.

Important Questions to Consider

Moses had to pass the baton because God had banned him from the Promised Land. Many of us have a hard time with that. And that's understandable. After all the faithfulness Moses displayed, after all the grumbling he endured, after all the suffering he went through because of obstinate Israel . . . he would not enter Canaan. He would die within sight of it. Seems unfair, doesn't it?

Let's deal with that question before we analyze the actual passing of the baton.

Why Couldn't Moses Enter Canaan?

Why did God hand down such a harsh judgment to Moses? In the same verse in which He declared that He would not allow Moses to enter the Promised Land, He provided His reasoning for His prohibition (20:12). Essentially, Moses had dishonored the Lord by deviating from His plan to provide water for the people at Meribah. He had drawn attention to himself instead of to God. He had obscured God's holiness and glory. He had allowed his frustration with the people to momentarily weaken his faith in God. So God told Moses he could not enter the Promised Land.

Who Qualified to Replace Moses?

In light of Moses' imminent departure, a second question naturally arose: Who was qualified to replace him? Only two candidates existed—Caleb and Joshua. Of all the people who took part in the Exodus, these men were the only two from the cursed generation whom God would allow to enter Canaan (14:30). And of these two, only Joshua had served as "the attendant of Moses from his youth" (11:28). Joshua naturally qualified as the best candidate to receive the leadership baton from Moses.

The Appointment of Moses' Successor

How, then, would this transition of leadership take place? Would Moses leave grudgingly—would the staff of leadership have to be pried from his hand? Or would he accept God's decision with obedience and humility? Let's see how things unfold.

Viewing the Land

The Israelites had been wandering the desert for forty years. Almost all the older generation was gone. Miriam had died (20:1). Aaron had died atop Mount Hor (vv. 23–29). Only Moses, Joshua and Caleb remained from the generation God had judged in the wilderness. And soon it would be Moses' time to pass from the scene. First, though, he would see the Promised Land.

> Then the Lord said to Moses, "Go up to this mountain of Abarim, and see the land which I have given to the sons of Israel. When you have seen it,

you too will be gathered to your people, as Aaron your brother was; for in the wilderness of Zin, during the strife of the congregation, you rebelled against My command to treat Me as holy before their eyes at the water." (27:12–14a)

Seems a little cruel of God, doesn't it? He led Moses to a mountaintop and showed him the Promised Land—the place he had spent forty years pursuing. Then God reminded him that he'd never realize his goal because of one act of rebellion . . .

Moses stood on the top of Mount Arabim, also called Pisgah, and looked over the whole land of Canaan. He let his eyes wander in every direction. It was more beautiful than he could have imagined. He studied every curve of the hill country and sniffed the breeze for any hint of Lebanon's cedar-covered slopes. What a prize for the Hebrew people! A prize that they, not Moses, would soon possess. As he looked, smelled, listened, the words of the Lord came back to him, haunted him.

"When you have seen the land, you too will be gathered to your people, as Aaron your brother was."

Moses remembered when Aaron was "gathered to his people." It had occurred over a year earlier. In the early morning, he, Aaron, and Aaron's son Eleazar ascended Mount Hor. First, the three men sat and looked out over the tents of the people. After a little while, Moses gently removed Aaron's priestly garments and put them on Eleazar, just as the Lord had commanded. Aaron died there atop Mount Hor, and Moses and Eleazar descended the mountain. The people wept for a month, and Moses mourned with them for all those days.

Now it was nearing Moses' turn. He continued to gaze at the land he had been pursuing for so long. Images of God's faithful presence with Israel flowed across his mind in a steady stream, like the Jordan River that he would never cross. Crimson lamb's blood dripping from doorposts. The screams of Egyptian soldiers suddenly silenced by the thunderous roar of the Red Sea's falling water. The wilderness floor crusted over with manna. The sonorous voice of God as He gave His Ten Commandments and all His Laws to Moses. The tabernacle, brimming with the blazing glory of the Lord. People writhing in the sand, dying from serpent venom and straining to catch a glimpse of their only salvation—a bronze serpent Moses had fastened to a pole.

So numerous were the ways God had blessed His people, Moses couldn't recall them all. He wasn't even aware of some of them until later, such as the prophet Balaam's public blessing of Israel before a Moabite king who had, ironically, hired the prophet to curse Israel. God had done so much. Could He not now rescind the punishment of His servant?

"Oh Lord God," Moses pleaded. "You have begun to show Your servant Your greatness and Your strong hand; for what god is there in heaven or on earth who can do such works and mighty acts as Yours? Let me, I pray, cross over and see the fair land that is beyond the Jordan, that good hill country and Lebanon."

But the Lord's anger burned against Moses for even asking.

> "Enough!" Yahweh commanded. "Speak to me no more of this matter. . . . You shall not cross over this Jordan."
>
> Moses, painfully accepting God's decision, sat and listened as the Lord continued to speak to him, instructing him about the leader who would take his place—Joshua.[1]

The Lord's actions seem cruel, but nothing could be further from the truth. Bringing Moses to the top of Mount Arabim was, in fact, an act of mercy. Moses, although he would never set foot on the land, would want to know that God had kept His promise to the people. He needed the reassurance that Canaan really existed and that God would give that land to the Hebrews. God mercifully allowed Moses to see this fulfilled promise with his own eyes and know that the last forty years of his life were not spent in vain.

Moses had brought the people to the Promised Land. Now someone else would have to take them in. A military leader. A warrior. Taking possession of the land would involve more than just pitching tents. Perhaps, as Moses perused the landscape, he noticed smoke rising from fires. Maybe he saw herds or flocks. Certainly he saw some evidence of habitation, some sign of the people who already possessed the land and would not like the idea of losing their homes to desert wanderers who worshiped a strange god.

Choosing the Man

Moses' response to the Lord reveals that he realized the people's need for a new leader.

> Then Moses spoke to the Lord, saying, "May the Lord, the God of the spirits of all flesh, appoint a man over the congregation, who will go out and

1. This dramatic narrative is based on words and events recorded in Numbers 20:23–29 and Deuteronomy 3:23–29.

come in before them, and who will lead them out
and bring them in, so that the congregation of the
Lord will not be like sheep which have no shepherd." (vv. 15–17)

The fact that Moses could not enter the land did not fill him
with self-pity. Instead, his concern turned to the Hebrew people.
Surprisingly, Moses didn't try to select his successor. Rather, he let
God choose; and the Lord selected a very special person—a man
close to Moses' heart.

So the Lord said to Moses, "Take Joshua the son of
Nun, a man in whom is the Spirit, and lay your hand
on him; and have him stand before Eleazar the priest
and before all the congregation, and commission
him in their sight." (vv. 18–19)

By laying his hand on Joshua, Moses conferred his authority on
him. Through this ceremony, the Israelites understood that Joshua
held the reins of leadership and therefore should be obeyed (v. 20).

Following the Plan

Moses did just as the Lord commanded him; and he
took Joshua and set him before Eleazar the priest
and before all the congregation. Then he laid his
hands on him and commissioned him, just as the
Lord had spoken through Moses. (vv. 22–23)

Moses harbored no bitterness. Once he knew God's choice, he
took the necessary steps to see God's man officially and publicly
placed into service.

Timeless Principles for Transferring Leadership

This chapter reveals a pivotal point in Israel's history. It describes a crucial exchange of power from an aging leader to a powerful warrior. Although our experiences today come on a much
smaller scale, we too experience changes in leadership. We can benefit from three of the timeless truths contained in Numbers 27:12–23.

First, *when God removes, He replaces.* The Lord never runs out
of potential servants. We should realize that His purposes are bigger
than any one person, and we should be open and sensitive enough
to recognize His replacements.

Second, *when God appoints, He approves*. God wants to bless the work of His new leaders. Even though we may struggle to adapt to the new leader's personality and methods, we need to remain open-minded, flexible, and hardworking. We should recognize God's sovereignty in putting that leader over us. And we should pray and work for the success of that person's ministry.

Third, *when God sustains, He gives success*. As long as God's leaders submit to His Spirit, their work will bear fruit for Him. We can help promote and maintain that success by praying for our new leaders, and by giving to them and cooperating with them.

 Living Insights

Leadership is like a relay race—it's often won or lost in the passing of the baton. We've studied the transition from Moses to Joshua. Now look at your own life. Have you seen God remove, appoint, or sustain Christian leaders? Has God ever appointed you as a leader in a ministry? Write out some of your observations on how God has fulfilled the timeless principles in your life or someone else's.

When God removes, He replaces.

_____

_____

When God appoints, He approves.

_____

_____

When God sustains, He gives success.

_____

_____

Now that you've done this, take some time to pray for these truths to become reality in your life or in the lives of those who are leading you.

Chapter 21

OBITUARY OF A HERO
Deuteronomy 34

The time was drawing near. The new census for Israel's army had been taken, laws for a settled rather than nomadic life were in place, Joshua was poised to lead the people into the Promised Land. And Moses would soon die.

Moses . . . die? What would Israel do without him? It was unimaginable. He had always been there—facing down Pharaoh, leading them through the Red Sea, interceding when their parents' complaints brought God's judgment, standing between them and the terrifying presence of the Lord at Mount Sinai. Like the ever-present pillar of cloud, Moses' faithfulness had been a beacon of hope and guidance throughout these long years of wandering.

What would become of Israel without Moses?

Moses may have been wondering the same thing. Not because he thought he was indispensable; Yahweh surely would be with the people and could accomplish His plans without him. But Moses knew how forgetful of God's goodness the people could be. How ungrateful for His care. How unresponsive to His love.

So, in his last act as their leader, Moses reminded them of where they had come from and why, where they were going and why. He explained God's holy and compassionate Law to them again and renewed God's covenant with them. He also reminded them of the blessings that would follow their total commitment to Yahweh—and the curses that would result from faithless disobedience. But most of all, throughout the three sermons given over his last forty days, Moses stressed God's gracious and faithful love of His people, to whom He was giving the Promised Land. This is what Moses' fifth and final book, Deuteronomy, is all about.

> For you are a people holy to the Lord your God. The Lord your God has chosen you out of all the peoples on the face of the earth to be his people, his treasured possession.
>
> The Lord did not set his affection on you and choose you because you were more numerous than other peoples, for you were the fewest of all peoples. But it was because the Lord loved you and kept the

oath he swore to your forefathers that he brought you out with a mighty hand and redeemed you from the land of slavery, from the power of Pharaoh, king of Egypt. Know therefore that the Lord your God is God; he is the faithful God, keeping his covenant of love to a thousand generations of those who love him and keep his commands. (Deut. 7:6–9 niv)

Now Moses had done all he could to prepare this new generation to enter the land and live for God. Now he could go home and live forever in the presence of his Lord.

Moses' Final Journey

Like many of the other monumental events in Moses' life, his death also took place on a mountaintop.

Now Moses went up from the plains of Moab to Mount Nebo, to the top of Pisgah, which is opposite Jericho.[1] (34:1a)

Moses climbed to the highest tip of Mount Nebo, which stands among the Abarim mountains and rises high above the rest of the range. Its summit provides a spectacular view, so from this vantage point, the Lord showed Moses all of the Promised Land.

And the Lord showed him all the land, Gilead as far as Dan, and all Naphtali and the land of Ephraim and Manasseh, and all the land of Judah as far as the western sea, and the Negev and the plain in the valley of Jericho, the city of palm trees, as far as Zoar. Then the Lord said to him, "This is the land which I swore to Abraham, Isaac, and Jacob, saying, 'I will give it to your descendants'; I have let you see it with your eyes, but you shall not go over there." (vv. 1b–4)

What a breathtaking sight! But what bittersweet emotions. On

---

1. Did Moses visit two locations—Pisgah and Nebo? Actually, the term "Pisgah" does not refer to a specific location but describes a special type of rock formation—a ridge or cleft. In this case, it indicates the summit of Mount Nebo. See Earl S. Kalland, "Deuteronomy," in *The Expositor's Bible Commentary*, gen. ed. Frank E. Gaebelein (Grand Rapids, Mich.: Zondervan Publishing House, 1992), vol. 3, p. 234.

one hand, Moses looked upon the fruition of his life's work and rested in the assurance that his people would take possession of the land he had led them to. On the other hand, he knew he would never set foot upon that land.

Perhaps Moses reminisced about all that he and the Israelites had gone through to reach the place where he now stood. The plagues in Egypt and the parting of the Red Sea. The golden calf and the bronze serpent. The legions of people who had died. The Hebrews had endured it all and, finally, had made it to the borders of the land of promise. Certainly he thought of God's faithfulness in fulfilling His covenant with the patriarchs Abraham, Isaac, and Jacob through this generation of their descendants.

This moment in which Moses surveyed the land must have held an emotional significance like few other moments in his life. And with the goodness of God as the last thing he saw, Moses passed away.

> So Moses the servant of the Lord died there in the
> land of Moab, according to the word of the Lord.
> (v. 5)

No farewells. No fanfare. He simply laid down, and the Lord took his spirit. Moses died alone, without family or friends standing at his side, holding his hand as he took his last breath. But Moses died secure, for the Lord remained with him. Moses died forever safe in the loving arms of God. Yahweh's timing came, and Moses' days ended. So God collected Moses' life into His embrace and took him home, burying His servant's body Himself.

> And He buried him in the valley in the land of
> Moab, opposite Beth-peor; but no man knows his
> burial place to this day. (v. 6)

There were no solemn processions; there was no stately funeral. Rather, the Lord buried Moses privately, ensuring that he "left behind him not a place of pilgrimage but an example of faith and obedience and a definitive word to follow."[2]

Moses' Lasting Legacy

At the time of his death, Moses was 120 years old (v. 7a)—

---

2. Ian Cairns, *Deuteronomy: Word and Presence*, International Theological Commentary series (Grand Rapids, Mich.: William B. Eerdmans Publishing Co., 1992), p. 305.

he'd lived through twelve decades of hope and hardship. Forty years as an Egyptian prince, forty years of obscurity in Midian, forty years leading a caravan of grumblers through the desert. Yet despite all his burdens and years, by God's grace "his eye was not dim, nor his vigor abated" (v. 7b). God supplied him with the stamina to lead His people. And he led them well.

When the Israelites learned that Moses had passed away, they mourned for him as they had for Aaron.

> So the sons of Israel wept for Moses in the plains of Moab thirty days. (v. 8a)

He would continue to live in the hearts and minds of Israel. And their devotion was justified. After all, Moses had constantly manifested his commitment to them by serving with a selfless dedication no other prophet, until Christ Himself, would match.

> Since that time no prophet has risen in Israel like Moses, whom the Lord knew face to face, for all the signs and wonders which the Lord sent him to perform in the land of Egypt against Pharaoh, all his servants, and all his land, and for all the mighty power and for all the great terror which Moses performed in the sight of all Israel. (vv. 10–12)

Other prophets would hear God's voice and receive His revelations, but only Moses had a face-to-face relationship with God. And only Christ has seen the Father and revealed Him fully to us (see John 1:17–18; Col. 1:15, 19; Heb. 3:3).

Life after Moses

What would Israel do without Moses? God had provided a new leader for them, a faithful man who was trained by Moses himself.

> Now Joshua the son of Nun was filled with the spirit of wisdom, for Moses had laid his hands on him; and the sons of Israel listened to him and did as the Lord had commanded Moses. (Deut. 34:9)

The days of wandering were over. It was time to enter the land of God's promise.

*J*oshua stood on a hill overlooking the Jordan River. Thirty days had passed since Moses' death, and the northern rains were swelling the river to an impassable flood. The overcast sky diffused the daylight and dimmed the bright colors of Canaan with dingy gray tones.

The land across the Jordan not only flowed with milk and honey but also teemed with warriors and giant men. But Joshua was not afraid of them; the Lord would fight Israel's battles, just as He had done before. No, Joshua was more concerned about his own people.

How would they respond to his leadership? He could never be Moses; he could never live up to that standard. Joshua dropped to the ground to pray. As his knees hit the earth, he recognized the voice of God.

"Joshua," the Lord said, "My servant Moses is dead. But I want you to take all these people, cross this Jordan, and take the land I'm giving them, just as I said to Moses. Everything from the Euphrates to the Mediterranean will be yours. No man, for all your days, will be able to stand against you. Just as I've been with Moses, so I will be with you. I will never disappoint or abandon you. So take courage and be strong—and walk in all the ways Moses taught you. Obey all of My laws and then you will have success."

Joshua remembered the scrolls Moses had entrusted to him. They were the treasure of Israel.

"Is it not I, the Lord, who has commanded you? Be strong and courageous! Don't tremble with fear, for I, the Lord your God, am with you wherever you go."

Joshua rose to his feet with his head high and shoulders back. The Lord's words had infused his spirit with unquenchable courage. He descended the hill to gather the officers and conquer the land for God.

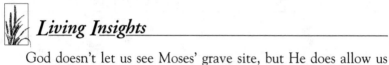

Living Insights

God doesn't let us see Moses' grave site, but He does allow us to read the Spirit's epitaph. If you were to sum up Moses' life, write his obituary, so to speak, what would you say? From our previous chapters, what are his strengths? His weaknesses? What contributions did he make? What has his relationship with God taught us? What legacies has he left behind?

_____

_____

_____

_____

_____

_____

_____

_____

_____

_____

_____

When you die, how would you like people to remember you? What words would you like inscribed on your tombstone? What accomplishments and character traits would you like to memorialize you?

_____

_____

_____

_____

_____

_____

_____

_____

Are you living in such a way that the above qualities will characterize your life? If not, what will you do this moment to start establishing your memorial?

_____

_____

_____

_____

_____

_____

_____

_____

Chapter 22

MOSES' FAITH, MOSES' CHOICES . . . AND ME

Hebrews 11:24–28

One of the most fascinating halls of fame is The Texas Ranger Hall of Fame and Museum in Waco, Texas. As visitors peruse the glass cases and exhibits, they encounter historical treasures such as Billy the Kid's 1873 Winchester Carbine taken from him by Sheriff Pat Garrett. They can also view firearms and possessions belonging to the notorious 1930s bank robbers Bonnie Parker and Clyde Barrow that were seized by legendary Ranger Frank Hamer.

The museum, in addition to displaying important artifacts, also memorializes thirty Rangers who have served the law with great distinction or even given their lives in the line of duty. By paying tribute to these elite cowboy lawmen, the Texas Ranger Museum captures the true purpose of a hall of fame—to identify people and display objects which have contributed to a beloved field or discipline.

One of the most important halls of fame in the world identifies people of whom we have no pictures or artifacts to display. This hall of fame is actually a "hall of faith." Located in Hebrews 11, this "museum" recounts the great heroes of our spiritual heritage, memorializing people who gave their lives for God or served Him with great distinction.

In our study of Moses' life, we have seen him be born to a cruelly oppressed people and die in sight of a free land of Israel's own. But to fully appreciate the life and times of this great servant of God, we have one more stop to make. Let's take one last look at Moses' life—the view that Hebrews' hall of faith affords us. There we'll see the choices that marked him as a faithful man of God, and through those choices, we'll learn how to improve our own walk with the Lord.

The Backdrop: Egypt

When the author of Hebrews lingers over Moses' life, he focuses

---

This message was not part of the original series but is compatible with it.

not on Midian, Sinai, or the wilderness but on Egypt. Why Egypt? Because it was the crucible of Moses' faith. Egypt was the greatest empire of that day, the pinnacle of culture, learning, power. F. B. Meyer helps us picture the land in which Moses was born and raised.

What a magnificent land must Egypt have been in those days of which Herodotus and the hiero-glyphic records speak! The atmosphere was rainless; the Nile brought from afar the rich alluvial soil, that bore corn enough to feed the world; the banks of the river were covered with cities, villages, stately temples, and all the evidences of an advanced civ-ilization; whilst mighty pyramids and colossal figures towered to a hundred feet in height. Seven millions of people throve on this green riband of territory; and whilst the great mass of them were probably poor and ignorant, the upper classes, and especially the priests, were remarkable for their familiarity with much of which we boast ourselves to-day.[1]

The Egyptian empire was certainly the jewel of the ancient world, and it undoubtedly shaped Moses during the first forty years of his life. Just as important as the culture, however, was the training he received and the position he held. While growing up in Egypt, Moses maintained the highest level of academic achievement. But Moses was more than just a student.

He was a statesman and a soldier. Stephen tells us that he was "mighty in words and in deeds": mighty in words—there is the statesman; mighty in deeds—there is the soldier. Josephus says that whilst he was still in his early manhood the Ethiopians invaded Egypt, routed the army sent against them, and threatened Memphis. In the panic the oracles were consulted; and on their recommendation Moses was entrusted with the command of the royal troops. He immediately took the field, surprised and defeated the enemy, captured their principal city, "the swamp-engirdled city of Meroë," and returned to Egypt

1. F. B. Meyer, *Moses: The Servant of God* (Grand Rapids, Mich.: Zondervan Publishing House, 1953), p. 20.

laden with the spoils of victory.[2]

If Moses was such a prominent personage in Egyptian society, wouldn't he have a memorial or monument preserving his name throughout the ages? All the great rulers of Egypt left some indication of their power and prowess. But Egypt built no monuments to Moses. From the easternmost section of Sinai to the westernmost region of the Libyan plateau, you won't find a single sign of him.

But what the hot, arid sands of Egypt lack, Scriptures' hall of faith contains. It reveals why Moses is conspicuously absent from Egypt's history.

The Spotlight: Moses' Faith

Moses made three significant decisions that obliterated his name from Egypt's records and enshrined him in the annals of God's people. Let's turn to Hebrews 11 and examine each of these choices.

He Sought God's Rewards instead of Egypt's Riches

> By faith Moses, when he had grown up, refused to be called the son of Pharaoh's daughter, choosing rather to endure ill-treatment with the people of God than to enjoy the passing pleasures of sin, considering the reproach of Christ greater riches than the treasures of Egypt; for he was looking to the reward. (vv. 24–26)

Notice that Moses made his decision when "he had grown up"— when he was mature. His was no rash impulse of youth; he thought it through, weighing the immediate consequences against the eternal rewards. For though Egypt had staggering wealth, and though all that his people had then was bondage, Moses trusted in God's promise to Abraham to make his descendants a great nation that would bless all the nations of the earth. So, by faith, he turned a cold shoulder to Egypt's scepter and the temporal pleasures of a pagan lifestyle to take hold of God's staff instead. He chose to walk the path of God, refusing the privileges of an earthly prince.

How, we may wonder, could Moses have considered "the reproach of Christ" when Jesus had not come yet? "Although Moses' understanding of the details of the Messianic hope was extremely

2. Meyer, Moses: The Servant of God, p. 21.

limited, he chose to be associated with the people through whom that hope was to be realized."[3] Bearing ill treatment for the Savior of the world was to him a small price to pay for a glorious eternity in God's presence.

He Left in Faith Rather Than in Fear

> By faith he left Egypt, not fearing the wrath of the king; for he endured, as seeing Him who is unseen. (v. 27)

Was Moses some kind of superman—never afraid, always victorious in faith? Our study has taught us better than that. When Moses broke up the two Hebrew slaves who were fighting and they brazenly taunted him about the Egyptian taskmaster he had killed, he was indeed afraid (Exod. 2:11–14). Afraid that he had misread God's timing for deliverance; afraid of what he had done. The Exodus account does not say expressly whether he was afraid of someone, nor does it say that he fled Pharaoh out of fear. In light of this Hebrews passage, we would be wrong to jump to such conclusions.

Rather, Moses left for Midian, where he "endured" or persevered in the faith that God would use him yet in some way to deliver His people.

He Followed God's Directions

> By faith he kept the Passover and the sprinkling of the blood, so that he who destroyed the firstborn might not touch them. (Heb. 11:28)

We often forget that Moses performed the first Passover without any tradition to fall back on. No one had ever done anything like it before. But he believed God's word; he believed that the blood sacrifice that God commanded would cover their sins and be their salvation in that long night of Egypt's judgment.

Houselights Up: Moses' Choices and You

Moses' faith can teach us many things, including these three principles that can buttress our own faith if we diligently apply them.

3. Philip E. Hughes and Donald W. Burdick, note on Hebrews 11:26, in *The NIV Study Bible*, gen. ed. Kenneth L. Barker (Grand Rapids, Mich.: Zondervan Bible Publishers, 1985), p. 1873.

First, *to have the discernment it takes to refuse the sinful, faith must overcome our feelings.* We must remember that sin's pleasures are only passing, but its consequences can last a lifetime. The life of faith, however, may yield "momentary, light affliction," but it produces "an eternal weight of glory far beyond all comparison" (2 Cor. 4:17).

Second, *to have the determination it takes to leave the familiar, faith must become our security.* When Moses walked out of Pharaoh's palace to join his people, he must have felt like he was walking off the face of the earth. With every step he made, however, God provided a sure footing upon which to stand. To have the courage to leave our familiar towns, jobs, and routines—if God is calling us to do so—we must stop looking at what we can see and begin trusting in the Lord we know.

Third, *to have the discipline it takes to do the unusual, faith must overshadow our critics.* Critics are a fact of life, especially for people who step out in faith. Moses certainly had his share of them. To follow the Lord, we must trust Him more than we fear those who would mock us.

Moses may never have had a monument raised to perpetuate his name in Egypt, but his place in the hall of faith is far better. "To this day," commentator Leon Morris notes,

> Moses is honored throughout the world, whereas the great ones who undoubtedly scoffed at his decision are completely forgotten. Even the name of Pharaoh's daughter is not known.[4]

God is a sure rewarder of those who seek and follow Him by faith.

 Living Insights

Moses was man of passion, of principle, of faith. Not a perfect man, but certainly a man devoted to God. As we wrap up our study on his life, take some time to reflect on and record what you've learned.

---

4. Leon Morris, *Hebrews*, Bible Study Commentary Series (Grand Rapids, Mich.: Zondervan Publishing House, Lamplighter Books, 1983), p. 112.

What about Moses has impacted you most? Why?

_____

_____

_____

_____

_____

What has his faith taught you?

_____

_____

_____

_____

_____

Have you identified with any of his frailties? His fears or frustrations, for example, or the times when everything felt like too
much? What encouragement did you find in how God helped him?

_____

_____

_____

_____

What have you learned from the Israelites? Do you feel less
prone to grumble? More apt to obey God from the heart? What
stands out in your mind as you think back on their behavior?

_____

_____

_____

_____

How has this study affected your view of God? For example what have you learned about His faithfulness?

_____

_____

_____

_____

_____

His provision and care for His people?

_____

_____

_____

_____

His holiness?

_____

_____

_____

_____

His promises?

_____

_____

_____

_____

have you seen Christ revealed in Moses' life?

_____

_____

_____

_____

_____

_____

_____

_____

_____

As significant as Moses is, the eyes of our hearts need to look beyond him to the Lord who sent him. For God was communicating through Moses His desire to have a relationship with His people. And He still has that desire today. Only He doesn't come through Moses now but through Christ. Spend some time with the Lord to look at your relationship with Him. And may Peter's words, which echo the words God gave Moses, focus your thoughts and lift your heart to the God who has chosen and saved you.

> But you are a chosen race, a royal priesthood, a holy nation, a people for God's own possession, so that you may proclaim the excellencies of Him who has called you out of darkness into His marvelous light. (1 Pet. 2:9)

BOOKS FOR
PROBING FURTHER

$\mathbf{M}$oses was a man of selfless dedication.

He left the comforts of Egyptian royalty to champion his en-slaved people. He accepted his exile in Midian and raised a family. And finally, he led the Hebrews through the wilderness even though they complained to him almost every step of the way.

Hopefully, you've come to know Moses more personally—to see him as a real flesh-and-bone man. If you'd like to know him better or learn more about the lessons drawn from his life, the following books will help you in your quest.

Commentaries

Childs, Brevard S. *The Book of Exodus: A Critical, Theological Com-mentary*. Philadelphia, Pa.: Westminster Press, 1974.

Cole, R. Alan. *Exodus: An Introduction and Commentary*. Reprint, Downers Grove, Ill.: InterVarsity Press, 1974.

Durham, John I. *Exodus*. Word Biblical Commentary series. Vol. 3. Waco, Tex.: Word Books, Publisher, 1987.

Gaebelein, Frank E., gen. ed. *The Expositor's Bible Commentary*. Vols. 2 and 3. Grand Rapids, Mich.: Zondervan Publishing House, Academic and Professional Books, 1990, 1992.

Hamilton, Victor P. *Handbook on the Pentateuch*. Grand Rapids, Mich.: Baker Book House, 1982.

Walvoord, John F. and Roy B. Zuck, eds. *The Bible Knowledge Com-mentary*. Old Testament edition. Wheaton, Ill.: Scripture Press Publications, Victor Books, 1985.

Youngblood, Ronald F. *Exodus*. Everyman's Bible Commentary Se-ries. Chicago, Ill.: Moody Press, 1983.

Topical Studies

Chafer, Lewis Sperry. *He That Is Spiritual: A Classic Study of the*

.l Doctrine of Spirituality. Rev. ed. Grand Rapids, Mich.: *.*lervan Publishing House, Academie Books, 1967.

., Bill. *Honest to God? Becoming an Authentic Christian.* Grand *.*apids, Mich.: Zondervan Publishing House, 1990.

*.*rson, Eugene H. *A Long Obedience in the Same Direction: Discipleship in an Instant Society.* Downers Grove, Ill.: InterVarsity Press, 1980.

Stanley, Charles. *How to Listen to God.* Nashville, Tenn.: Thomas Nelson Publishers, Oliver-Nelson Books, 1985.

Swindoll, Charles R. *Dropping Your Guard: The Value of Open Relationships.* Waco, Tex.: Word Books, Publisher, 1983.

Wald, Oletta. *The Joy of Discovery in Bible Study.* Rev. ed. Minneapolis, Minn.: Augsburg Publishing House, 1975.

Wangerin, Walter, Jr. *The Book of God: The Bible as a Novel.* Grand Rapids, Mich.: Zondervan Publishing House, 1996.

Yancey, Philip. *Disappointment with God: Three Questions No One Asks Aloud.* Grand Rapids, Mich.: Zondervan Publishing House, 1988.

Some of the books listed may be out of print and available only through a library. For those currently available, please contact your local Christian bookstore. Books by Charles R. Swindoll may be obtained through Insight for Living, as well as some books by other authors.

Insight for Living also offers study guides on many books of the Bible, as well as on a variety of issues and Bible characters. For more information, see the ordering instructions that follow and contact the office that serves you.

Ordering Information

Moses

If you would like to order additional study guides, purchase the cassette series that accompanies this guide, or request our product catalogs, please contact the office that serves you.

United States and International locations:

Insight for Living
Post Office Box 69000
Anaheim, CA 92817-0900

1-800-772-8888, 24 hours a day, 7 days a week
(714) 575-5000, 8:00 A.M. to 4:30 P.M., Pacific time, Monday to Friday

Canada:

Insight for Living Ministries
Post Office Box 2510
Vancouver, BC, Canada V6B 3W7

1-800-663-7639, 24 hours a day, 7 days a week

Australia:

Insight for Living, Inc.
General Post Office Box 2823 EE
Melbourne, VIC 3001, Australia

(03) 9877-4277, 8:30 A.M. to 5:00 P.M., Monday to Friday

World Wide Web:
www.insight.org

Study Guide Subscription Program

Study guide subscriptions are available. Please call or write the office nearest you to find out how you can receive our study guides on a regular basis.